C000068020

To Frances Hanson for providing the idea and my daughter Sally-Anne for all her help producing the copy for this book.

John Hanson Jnr.

THE MOTORING ADVENTURES OF A BABY BOOMER

AUSTIN MACAULEY PUBLISHERS™

LONDON · CAMBRIDGE · NEW YORK · SHARJAH

A CIP catalogue record for this title is available from the British Library.

ISBN 9781398467163 (Paperback)
ISBN 9781398467170 (ePub e-book)

www.austinmacauley.com

First Published 2022
Austin Macauley Publishers Ltd ®
1 Canada Square
Canary Wharf
London
E14 5AA

Book Cover Notes

John Hanson eventually became a successful London lawyer, but he did his best to postpone this result for a long as possible.

First, he travelled the UK with his itinerant singing father, John Hanson Snr, known for his fine tenor voice and dashing presence in operettas like the Desert Song. Then, unprepared to leave the Bedouin travelling lifestyle, he enjoyed 12 years visiting the outback regions of Australia. In particular, he explored the wilds of Northern Australia working as a lawyer just 12 months after Darwin had been wiped out by a cyclone. The law took on a different meaning, acting for crocodile hunters, crocodile surveying academics, aboriginals, miners, cattlemen and all the colourful characters of the Northern Territory.

As middle age beckoned, he moved back to London and still travelled the world as an international lawyer. All the time, the motor car played an important part, typical of the post-war baby boomer.

This book is an unfashionable appreciation of the combustion engine and the freedom it provided to several generations irrespective of wealth and status.

Preface

As I bought yet another motor vehicle, I asked myself: "What is it about this method of transport that has caused me to purchase 68 cars in 68 years…and counting?"

Certainly, my children have not inherited the interest (far from it and the future does not omen well for the keen driver). However, born in 1952, I am a child of the combustion engine. The following 50 years provided car enthusiasts with the greatest choice and opportunity to express their personality. The motor car allowed personal freedom and, within financial limits, multiple choice of design.

Of course, many practical factors limit the choice as the motor car is dominated by its function. Is it needed for shopping, long-distance travel, load carrying, speed or simply for pure beauty? Therefore, it is rare, if ever, that one motor car can fulfil all of these functions equally well. This fact alone has led me, when I have had the cash and space, to buy multiple vehicles.

In retrospect, none have been highly priced, or vehicles valued by experts. I have always searched for vehicles which I thought others may have missed and were not overpriced. Therefore, they have never been new nor kept long enough to rise in value. I certainly never wanted a vehicle that was so rare and expensive that I would worry about it leaving the driveway. A viewer of the TV series 'Chasing Classics', the presenter, Wayne Carrini, regularly discovers Ferraris, Mercedes, Lamborghinis, and others which have been driven briefly and parked in barns and garages for 30 years. One Stutz Bearcat had been in storage for 85 years. Wayne was in ecstasy at the discovery. I considered it to be a waste of 85 years of driving; allowing a very special car to rust and rot.

It is true my rapid turnover of some vehicles has resulted in a failure to maximise value and made me a car dealer's prize customer. The best example may be a vehicle I bought in Australia in 1981, namely a 1972 Valiant Charger

E38 R/T, bought for the grand price of AUS$3,000 and now worth AUS$400,000. Well, you cannot win them all!

This is a very simple book; it is not a personal search for the psychological defect which has caused this buying excess! It is a farewell – a farewell to the freedom and joys provided by the motor car and a way of life. Hello Brave New World, alternative fuels, and driverless boxes. It is for those aficionados of a certain age who are looking back at some fun, in a lucky and interesting five decades.

This book is a personal celebration of engineered sculptures on the move and the journeys that they have taken me on – whether it be crossing the Nullarbor Plain in perhaps the worst car I ever owned or a commute up the M2 in an elderly Rolls-Royce. If on occasions, I drift away from cars into personal anecdotal material, I hope I only do so where it might be of interest or at least mildly amusing. This is an 'Auto'-biography of a different kind.

Chapter 1
A Family Motoring Heritage
(The Arrol-Aster Bluebird)

Both of my grandads were born into the car manufacturing centres of Britain – Coventry and Birmingham. Grandad Stokes was a Coventry man through and through, never moving from Earlsdon, apart from a brief venture as a hotelier after the Second World War. A cheerful chappie, happy on half a pint with his five brothers (and five sisters) – all bald pink-cheeked and 5ft 3in tall – he was a shop floor foreman for the Rootes factory in Coventry, manufacturing historic brands such as Hillman, Singer, and Sunbeam-Talbot. Sadly, by 1967, the huge Ryton plant had been taken over by Chrysler, an indication of Britain's failing motoring health. Later, it was taken over by Peugeot until closure in 2007.

Indeed, anyone born in Coventry in the twentieth century inherited a motor car gene. The industrial revolution had developed skills and crafts in the Midlands – first textile, then watch and clock-making and finally, bicycles as the cycling craze took off. As the region moved through these changes, there was confirmation that light industry only needed a skilled work force and bold management. One of these capitalists was nimble enough to stay ahead of these trends in the late nineteenth century, moving from bicycles to motorbikes to motor cars – the Riley family. At first, father William was reluctant to take the plunge but was persuaded by his four sons to manufacture the first vehicle in 1906. Riley remained an important name in British motoring until the 1940s with the family indulging in rallying and Le Mans. In 1934, Riley's four cars gained 2nd, 3rd, 6th and 13th place – the latter vehicle driven for the first time by a woman in the Le Mans, Dorothy Riley.

The city and industry were dominated by charismatic entrepreneurs like Captain Black (standard Triumph), William Lyons (SS Cars and later, Jaguar) and William and Reg Rootes (Hillman and Humber) moving from Kent. Other centres included Oxford (Morris), Birmingham (Austin) and the Ford Model T in Manchester. Captain Black, in particular, demonstrated all of the cavalier and piratical traits necessary for success in a new market. Coming from nowhere, he married into the Hillman motoring family. It did not prevent him from being head-hunted by Standard Triumph where he installed an assembly line increasing production from 8000 to 55,000 a year. He was flamboyant, confident and addicted to alcoholic binges.

In later years, he battled for local dominance with William Lyons whose sports cars and sports saloons had taken Coventry, the UK, and the world by storm. Starting with the SS Jaguar pre-Second World War, the 1950s was dominated chronologically by 120/140XK, the D-type race car (winner of Le Mans), the fabulous E-type, the MKI and MKII saloons, the MKX, S type, 420, 420 G and the XJ saloons. One winner after another until it almost fell afoul of nationalisation. Only re-privatisation saved the brand in 1984 under the reign of John Egan.

Grandad Watts was a fine-looking man from his photos but a man I never met. He was early in his adoption of motor engineering as an occupation learnt in Birmingham and in the army in the First World War. When the war was over, he plucked Grandma from the safety of her family and emigrated to Canada. He must have identified Oshawa, a Suburb of Toronto, as a potential source of work.

Back in 1907, in these early motoring days, the McLaughlin Motor Car Company had started manufacturing vehicles. By 1920, when Grandad and Grandma arrived, the Chevrolet Motor Car Co. of Canada had been formed and merged with General Motors to create General Motors of Canada.

So, Grandad had found gainful employment in difficult times and with the new addition of a son, John, my father, contemporary photographs show a happy little family indulging in corn picnics in the fields. John was later to become John Hanson, adopting Grandma's surname, and became one of the best-known light opera tenors on stage and radio in the 1950s.

Sadly, my lovely, but fragile, Grandma suffered badly from a heart condition which could not withstand the harsh Canadian winter. Therefore, after a mere five years, the family returned home. However, in the mid-1920s home did not provide any obvious employment for Grandad so, of all unlikely places for a motor engineer, the family settled in the bucolic countryside outside Dumfries.

He joined a car manufacturer with some historic credibility, being known for making the first automobile in the UK in 1898 – the Arrol Johnston Dogcart. The short-lived Scottish automobile industry failed to develop but continued to show invention with Arrol-Johnston, despite near bankruptcy, commissioning the first factory in Britain using concrete and reinforced metal in Heathall, Dumfries. By 1929, Grandad had joined the company as final inspector, now merged with Aster of Wembley. Surely, he must have loved his involvement in the company's remodelling and refabrication of Captain Malcolm Campbell's (later to be knighted) record attempting car – the third Bluebird. Despite the new bodywork, the engine remained untouched and had been superseded by competitors. The captain failed to surpass Henry Seagrave's record when the attempt was made in South Africa.

Amazingly, for a grandson who was never to meet his grandad, British Pathe News covered the fabrication of the Arrol-Aster Bluebird and provide an excellent film of a tall engineer foreman in overalls directing and assisting proceedings. Grandad appears clearly in every frame (YouTube the Bluebird 1929). He also test drove the Bluebird III (or so Dad said). Grandad Watts waited until I reached 68 years old to jump from the Pathe News film like a spectre to delight me and I saw him move for the first time. It was oddly touching.

The family remained poor despite continuous employment for Grandad. However Arrol-Aster shortly closed down leaving him to take the best job on offer as a works manager at a large petrol station. He would have moved back to Coventry but for Dad's education.

Chapter 2
Touring the Provinces

This little Dumfries family eked out a living in difficult times. The 'Singing Fool' (as Dad was nicknamed at school) was lucky enough to receive a free scholastic Scottish education at the Dumfries Academy where his talent is still celebrated on the school gates. The education was the best available in the UK for the son of a working man in the 1930s. He proved to be far from foolish. However, Dad's USP was always his voice. At the age of 11, he was broadcasting from BBC Scottish regional radio as a boy soprano and referred to as 'the well-known Dumfries boy singer' with a 'remarkable voice'. So, at 11 years old he was paid as a professional.

In 1932, on a rare holiday in Coventry at 12 years old, he featured in several concerts given by Charles Chadwell and his Orchestra at the Coventry Hippodrome. The Hippodrome, rebuilt as an art deco Palace in 1936, survived a direct bomb hit, staged the 'Wings for Victory' concert in 1943 to raise local spirits during the Coventry blitz. Again, Charles Chadwell led the BBC Hippodrome Orchestra.

At 16, Dad received an offer to join Chadwell as a singer with the band and he even received an offer from an unknown benefactor to travel to Milan for operatic training at the Conservatoire of Milan. Then the Second World War happened. However, his mum and dad were not keen and so he was trained as a Post Office telephone inspector in Dumfries, a job he loathed. His parents' departure to Coventry and the proximity of the War allowed him to give up the day job and move South. After setting up a machine shop for the war effort, Grandad contracted tuberculosis. Later Dad also caught TB, preventing him from joining the RAF. Before the end of the war, Grandma died of a heart attack and Grandad had passed away. Dad would no doubt have joined them if he had not been lucky enough to be one of the first UK patients to be treated with penicillin in 1946.

Before the onset of illness, Dad had broadcast several times with Charles Chadwell, then he worked in the Morris Engines factory at the Courthouse Green, which had switched from making power units for Morris Cars to providing military vehicles for the War, including tanks. Later Dad was employed in production control at Hoburn Aero Components, a factory machining key parts for Bristol and Aero engines.

A move to London after the war allowed John Watts to become 'John Hanson', marry Brenda Stokes and start his singing career through concerts and numerous radio broadcasts. He became the most sought-after tenor in England, singing in radio broadcasts such as Songs for the Shows, Melody Time, Variety Bandbox, Workers Playtime and Rays a Laugh, the latter of which regularly had audiences in excess of 20 million. This variety show, hosted by the music hall comedian Ted Ray, gave starts to young performers such as Peter Sellers, Kenneth Williams, Spike Milligan, and Dad.

January 19, 1952 saw the birth of a 7lb boy in the Walton-on-Thames Cottage Hospital. It was not the era of fathers being around for the birth and in any event, Dad was broadcasting. The sex of the new baby was not known and so names had not been discussed. Somehow the Evening Standard (or News) heard about the miraculous conception before Dad and rushed to the hospital for a photo. Mum was put on the spot and asked for a name to publish. Unsurprisingly John was the first name to come into her head.

So, I became Johnnie to differentiate Junior from Senior without any input from Dad. He, on the other hand, celebrated with a song on the radio (dedicated t to his son) the old Paul Robeson favourite, 'Mighty Lak' A Rose'. Perhaps he should have added, 'when I finally see him'.

Sweetest little fellow, everybody knows
Don't know what to call him but he's mighty like a rose
Lookin' at his mammy with eyes so shiny blue
Make you think that heaven is comin' close to you

Actually, it is a song for a bass baritone and would have suited Grandad Watts better. He was a good and kind Dad but his actual involvement in my upbringing was sort of summed up by my initiation into the world – singing from a distance. No complaint – it is just how it is living with a performer.

The 1950s saw a change in musical taste requiring John Hanson Snr to become a 'Matinee Idol' reviving all the great 1920s' and 1930s' operetta, such as The Student Prince, The Vagabond King, Lilac Time, Maid of the Mountains, Glamorous Years but, first and foremost, the Desert Song.

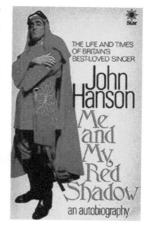

The Desert Song was first produced for the West End in 1927 and filmed several times subsequently. Dad's dark good looks and tenor voice suited flamboyant romantic roles such as the lead, The Red Shadow. His first revival was produced in 1954 touring the provinces, namely all the UK theatres bar the West End. Therefore, the motor car started to become a critical part of the family's life. The provincial tours lasted as long as 26 weeks and extended from Torquay to Glasgow, very rarely sticking to any geographical proximity. The car carried everything from nappies to evening suits and the family moved around the country like a Bedouin nomad caravan, stopping at various theatrical digs, in glorified boarding houses accommodating theatrical types on the annual tour. Mrs McKay in Manchester was perhaps the most well-known and considered her establishment to be preferable to any five-star hotel. It shows that Dad was a pretty affable fellow when he agreed to take our hamster and cage with us. Sadly, he made the mistake of placing his velvet collared overcoat over the cage which resulted in a very neat but unrepairable hole.

On another occasion, we stayed with a Swiss family in an enormous tenement flat in Glasgow near the botanical gardens. The budgerigar was called Pete and as soon as Dad walked into the flat, he jumped onto Dad's beautifully coiffured hair screaming 'I'm pretty Pete'. Dad loathed all pets as a matter of principle, but still refrained from squashing the little pest.

With all this weekly travel, comfort and reliability of our motor transport became critical. The first car was a Triumph Renown, a legacy of the 1930's design, which imitated the Bentley Standard Steel Sports Saloon. I remember it as being comfortable even at three years old but a review of its performance indicates that it had a 0 to 60mph of 25 seconds and a top speed of 77 mph. By 1957, Dad had decided he needed to move into the 1950s and bought a Ford Zodiac Mark II with its typical two-tone blue and white livery, the more luxurious version of the Ford Zephyr. At five years old, I was impressed by its

American-style tail-end and white wall tyres, glamorous vinyl, and chrome interior. Although considerably cheaper than the Renown, performance had improved to 0 to 60 and 17 seconds and a 10% improvement on the top speed. However, it still managed only 86bhp as it was restricted by a poor exhaust system.

It was probably during constant family touring that my Interest or obsession took hold. Some families indoctrinate children with belief codes, whether it be Christianity, Islam, or Hindu but my family introduced me, unknowingly, to the worship of the automobile. On the Christmas before my 3rd Birthday, Uncle Reg, a talented cabinet, and patent maker, had made me a lovely red and deep green wooden garage together with a forecourt and petrol pump! I remembered it sitting in the corner of Grandad Stokes dining room in their Victorian terraced house, surrounded by various smaller parcels which I ripped open (with a little help) and, to my joy, found them to be a variety of Dinky Toy miniature cars. They were diecast zinc alloy toys manufactured by Meccano between 1934 and 1979. For several years subsequently, wherever dad was performing, we drove back overnight to stay with Grandad and Grandma Stokes over Christmas. Every time I would receive more dinky toys so, as a result, the garage had to be transported around the country with us, with a larger and larger collection.

These journeys were tiresome for my younger sister and me. To while away the time, we sang 'car songs' and played games. My party piece was to name, at four years old, every car on the road. I was infallible, which Dad boasted about to his show 'Cast' and friends. Of course, journeys were longer before the advent of motorways. I remember clearly the trip to Coventry from Walton-on-Thames in Surrey, through Henley and Oxford. It sometimes took four hours despite the dearth of motor vehicles in the 1950s compared with the present day, licensed vehicle numbers only totalled five million in 1960. This may seem a lot to many but in 2019 the number totalled 39 million! Therefore, journeys were more pleasant for the passengers, but harassing for the driver. There were plenty of 'pit-stops', picnic stops and rests but life for the Hansons was shortly to change in 1957 with my schooling commencing at five years old.

Chapter 3
A Jaguar Lifestyle

With the advent of school, our family split in two for six days a week. Mum, Stella (my sister) and I stayed at home by the Thames in Walton, living a typical middle-class existence. By contrast, Dad continued to travel the land, producing, and appearing in various operetta, concerts, and broadcasts. Despite the lengthy distances involved, he sped back to us on a Saturday night; many times, arriving back as late as 4 p.m. Sunday was rest day, roast beef, and lemon meringue pie (Mum using Royal's filling) for Sunday lunch. Monday, Dad was off again early in the morning reinforced by supplies from Mum.

Therefore, the car became even more important with Dad driving as much as 40,000 miles per year. It shows how I became fixated by the motor car because I remember the purchase of the next car in 1959, perhaps because at seven years old I went to the showroom and the car was a Jaguar and thereafter Dad became a 'Jaguar Man' for the next 25 years. The car was the new Jaguar MK2 in Cotswold blue – a beautiful car and the 'latest thing'. As dad discovered, however, it was the wrong Jaguar MK2; the 2.4 model.

The purchase was made whilst Dad was performing a summer season in Morecombe Winter Gardens leading his company in the Student Prince and the Vagabond King where we had joined him, living at a small Heysham cottage. However, I was not around when, after nine months, he decided that the underperforming 2.4 Jag did not carry him home fast enough. Although faster than the Zodiac, it still struggled to achieve 100mph and had a 0-60 time of only three seconds better than the Zodiac.

By 1959, the M1 had just opened so speed became more relevant with the open roads, the limited number of cars and no speed limits. For a limited period, this became the best time to drive a car rapidly. This provided an excuse for Dad to upgrade the Jaguar to a white Jaguar MK2 3.4 with red leather upholstery – a glamour car for a romantic tenor. The increase of 90bhp from 120 to 210bhp brought the Jag into the modern era with a 0-60 time somewhere between 8–9 seconds and a top speed of 120 mph. He had in one purchase doubled the BHP and, noting this was 60 years ago, we have certainly not greatly improved the combustion engine over that period.

I can confirm the top speed as I clearly remember a trip back from Coventry on an empty M1 shortly after the purchase of the 3.4. I was eight years old, sitting in the plush leather back bench seat with Stella. Mum was in the front seat and Dad decided to find out how fast his new toy would go. As he put his foot down on the accelerator the speedometer was counted down to 120 mph with Mum's constant refrain of 'that was fast enough' but with the backseat passengers begging Dad to go faster. By 1965, this record-breaking run would not have been possible with speed limits introduced. I suspect Dad's midnight journeys rarely stuck to the limits, but he drove beautifully. I do not remember him ever having an accident – unlike his son.

The family continued to join their leading man during the holidays – sometimes an operetta and other times a summer season, or Dad's pet hate, a pantomime. Memories of the summer seasons remain fresh in the mind with six-eight weeks in a variety of seaside resorts including Morecombe, Southsea, Torquay, Eastbourne, Dublin, Paignton, and others.

By 1963, we had moved onto the last and best *Jaguar MK2 - the 3.8 litre*. Performance was only marginally increased by the additional 10bhp, but it looked splendid in vivid red with red upholstery and wire wheels, with whitewall tyres. It was virtually the same engine as the E-Type.

Life had now settled into a pattern with a restrained middle class lifestyle during term time – school and playing with neighbouring kids in our unmade cul-de-sac by the river. Another car had been introduced into the family with Mum passing her driving test and buying a pale blue Austin A35. It was never a car to inspire with a 1000cc engine allowing a 0-60 time of 30 seconds! I am sure it improved Mum's lot, but I had, from the age of six, used buses and feet to transport myself independently. Suddenly, I was picked up from school – the start of the school run! I missed my stopover in the sweet shop near the school, buying gobstoppers, sherbet lollipops and liquorice. Most of all, I missed browsing the bookshop and toy shop at the end of the bus route. I put down my pocket money on books in the Nelson and Collins Classics Editions together with airfix models and miniature soldiers at the Toy Shop. I was a self-contained little boy and enjoyed walking out of the back gate to the corner shop to buy a loaf of bread! Mum was now a driver and a Safeway's shopper so all this independence stopped but I was always self-reliant.

This is one of the downsides of the motor car in the last 50 years – it has actually reduced the freedom and independence of children. Do away with the school run and we could probably keep the petrol engine.

In the holidays we followed Dad's work unless he was 'resting'. Even his splendid vehicle purchases followed a routine every two years – he would part exchange his car for the latest saloon in the Jaguar range.

By 1965, the *Jaguar S Type* had entered the market with a 3.4 and 3.8 choice of engines. It was a combination of the huge *Jaguar MK X* and the smaller *MK2*, introducing the independent rear suspension. The design was probably not as pure due to this hybrid compromise with the MK2 front end and the MK X boxy rear. Also, performance was slightly compromised by the lack of room in the engine bay to fit a third carburettor. The interior also provided a compromise between the MK X and MK2 – more wood than one, less than the other.

The speed of design and the fact that Jaguar continued to manufacture all three vehicles meant that this model was one of the ugliest built by Jaguar. It is odd that, when creating a pastiche design for the 1999 Jaguar, the designers copied this design.

However, it did not put Dad off. He did not hold back opting for the top of the range, a *Jaguar S-type 3.8* in glistening red with red upholstery. Shortly after his purchase, Jaguar produced yet another saloon – the Jaguar 420. It was really yet another variant of the 3.8 MK2 and competed between 1966 and 1969 with its three relatives – with the MK2 3.8 disappearing and renamed the 250 and 320, the 420G, the S Type and the 420.

Performance was marginally increased in the Jaguar 420 with 245bhp, but all of these vehicles had similar roots. The design followed a squashed version of the 420G (Mark 10) but for a few years it was quite successful. However, both manufacturer and the car buyer were waiting for the revolutionary XJ6 which was to represent the Jaguar and Daimler design for many years to come.

None of this stopped Dad, of course, he had to buy the latest Jaguar 420 and 'guess what', it was covered in glistening red paint and a luscious red leather interior with even more wood!

Chapter 4
An Unusual Upbringing

It is not that easy to switch from one life to another on a termly basis. Usually, holidays were taken up following the show business caravan, but I can remember three overseas holidays which were unusual in the 1950s/1960s – Torremolinos, Majorca and Portugal. Even overseas – Dad could still not get away from his reputation and one incident, in particular, amused a 15-year-old but not his father. We were in a hotel lift when he was accosted by an 80-something elegant lady, 'You're the Red Shadow – 1927 West End'. This would have meant Dad was 40 years older than his years. She was clearly muddling Harry Welchman from the original show with Dad's 1967 performance at the Palace Theatre, London. The error was in a sense understandable because Mr Welchman also performed in the Vagabond King and the New Moon. It is the only time I thought Dad would tell a member of the public what he really thought but he did not even bother to correct her.

As I became older, I found that I could not be described as a typical middle-class child or a product of the show business lifestyle. In the 1960s and 1970s, there was no Hello Magazine or universal appreciation of 'FAME'. Fathers of my friends (and adult neighbours) were solicitors, stockbrokers, accountants, and businessmen. The entertainment career was not considered a 'real job'. At a party, at one of the neighbours the pompous host asked my father whether he could really make a living out of singing. This was at a time when Dad starred in the West End, made annual LPs, appeared on the radio and TV. Indeed, I suspect, he could have bought our obnoxious neighbour several times over. I was always amazed at how this courteous and modest man kept his temper.

My restricted number of friends were just as ignorant, but this had some advantages in my adolescence as I was generally left alone because I was considered different but not a bullying target. When younger, I really threw myself into the show business lifestyle when on Tour or staying by the seaside for a summer season. The Desert Song was my favourite Operetta because of the glamourous Arab clothes. I was allowed (before the days of health and safety) to dress up with the Red Shadow's headdress (reaching the floor) and mask, wielding a curved knife as a sword singing 'The Riff Song':

Over the ground
There was a sound
It is the drum, drum, drum of the hoofbeat in the sand
And all who plunder learn to understand to understand.
The cry of
Ho!
So, we sing as we are riding
Ho!
It's a tune you best be hiding low
It means the Riffs are abroad,
Go
Before you've bitten the sword...

OK, so it's not Bob Dylan but it was great for a five years old racing around the backstage corridors making the manager's life a misery. However, Manager Bob was my buddy and his partner, Dougie (a chorus boy and Dad's dresser for many years), were almost part of the family. Often Dad, being a hard worker, was also performing concerts on Sundays as well as eight performances of his weekly show. Mum used to go with him for company and leave my sister and me to be looked after by Bob and Dougie who produced and directed our Sunday afternoon concert. This required us to prepare a programme and dress up – my favourite act being our flamenco performance.

In the dressing room, there were certain show business rules and number one was 'No Whistling' and number two 'No Scavenging Dad's Supply of Chocolate Biscuits'. I was often put in the audience to count the number of punters and report back; I became pretty accurate to 100 customers. I was allowed at the side of the stage and became pals with the chorus who we met for coffee at about 11 a.m. most mornings. In the early days, it was usually the Kardomah chain if available. It was Dad's alternative to the post show dinner which his appalling stomach could not cope with.

The dressing room always contained certain aids for his singing voice, including Sanderson Throat Specific for clearing his throat and Neophren nasal spray for clearing his sinus. The dressing table was organised to spread out his pancake, eye liners and grease paint and other magical substances to put on his 'stage face'. Then, behind a screen, his stage clothes were added and instantly my dad became the Red Shadow, the Vagabond Kind, the Student Prince, and many other heroes for a little boy. On tour, we were all very much a gypsy family (including the cast and managers) moving from place to place as outsiders. I have felt like an outsider all of my life but have very much enjoyed that status – it made me a good objective lawyer.

School holidays were as unpredictable as term time was predictable. The stability of only two schools – preparatory and public school with the common entrance at 13. However, until 12 years old, I was a little wild; perhaps escaping from the benevolent dictatorship of my 5ft tall mum. At five years old, I ended up in hospital whilst throwing broken flowerpots outside Lower Remove. In strode, Mum to the Headmaster's study castigating him for lack of supervision whose response was, "Mrs Hanson, your son is no angel." Of course, she did not believe him despite breaking windows with my much-loved catapult and throwing stones at cars.

I indulged in gang warfare on the playing field. As a protection, to the bullying by the main gang, I gathered together similar victims in a reasonably successful attempt at resistance – I was always a good organiser but a modest pugilist. The only time Dad was able to come to a sporting event was the much-detested boxing competition. Organised by our weird gym teacher, whose greatest delight was to tickle our genitals with a leather strap when we were straddling gym equipment. Indeed, the teachers included a large maths teacher sacked for throwing a young boy through a glass window, a French teacher noted for requiring you to sit on his knee and a lesbian German and English couple renowned for necking out behind the bicycle shed. All the names are fixed in my mind, but they shall remain nameless.

Back to the boxing tournament – it was not a success. First the rope was too close to the wooden gym walls, if caught in a corner your head could be satisfactorily banged against the wall. I was matched against one of my primary bullying enemies who happened to be the best boxer in the school. With my head banging against the wall, the fight was stopped for tears. Subsequently, I was matched with someone against whom I could achieve the same result. So, what lesson did we learn – there is always someone who can beat you up and someone you can beat up!

A boxing bag was bought by Dad – that was his sole contribution to my athletic wellbeing. So, school life went on with few major successes or failures until at 12 years old, I followed the family tradition and caught Tuberculosis. Life changed immediately for everyone as I was exiled to bed for 12 months with daily visit from the District Nurse for penicillin injections and weekly visits from my teachers.

My only leisure consisted of my comics (the Hotspur and the Rover and Wizard) and books. However, academically my results improved hugely with no distractions. When I returned in time for Common Entrance I had moved to the top of my form and became House Captain. My Common Entrance results were all over 75%, which allowed me the choice of three fine schools – Westminster, Kings College Wimbledon and Cranleigh. I sometimes ponder if TB was the best thing that ever happened to me. I never looked back and always preferred to teach myself. My granddaughter has benefited in a similar fashion from working on-line during the Covid Crisis.

My hobbies were many and, without the distraction of modern technology, some would say old-fashioned, which included reading, music (classic to rock), stamp collecting (assisted by Dad's fans) and Art – particularly portraits of celebrities such as Rudolph Nuryev, Elizabeth Taylor, Joan Baez and Richard Burton in oils, pen and ink and charcoal. My little attic den was covered with hanging model aeroplanes and the floor with immaculately painted Airfix mini soldiers. My home from home was up a folding ladder, included my punch ball, a very mini snooker table and dart board.

All my boyhood, Mum made me work for my money. Pocket money was pitiful unless I augmented with, for example, my neighbour car washing scheme. She was determined nothing should come too easily and as I got older (and refused to follow the gypsy caravan) she insisted I had a holiday job – if I did not find one, she would, and it was not much fun getting up at 04:00 p.m. to work on the dustbins. As a student one was always the subject of practical jokes.

As a binman I was paired up with a 6ft 4in giant who came from the local Mental Institution on a work experience scheme. Conversation was limited but he was co-opted by the gang into encouraging me to lift up a bin (metal in those days) at the local engineering plant in Weybridge. I collapsed on the floor as I attempted to throw the bin on my shoulder – finding myself covered in iron filings. However, there was good news as much of the time was spent at cafes – breakfast at 07:00 a.m., coffee at 10:00 a.m., lunch at 01:00 p.m. and home by 02:00 p.m.!

The japes continued when on my first day as a labourer for a builder I was asked to break up a large area of reinforced concrete with a hammer and chisel – later augmented by powers drill and hammer. It was, of course, I who delivered the post at Christmas, and I always got the round which required a visit to the gypsy encampment and being chased by rabid dogs. It was the era of the 'Graduate', so I dreamt of being seduced by the experienced housewife – it never happened sadly.

The most fun, and dangerous, job was as a tree surgeon's assistant at Hampton Court. Unhappily many of the lovely trees had to be cut down because they were decimated by Dutch Elm Disease. Therefore, they needed an influx of cheap and very unskilled labour – primarily students. We were using chain saws, 7lb axes (one of which I put through the toe of my heavy-duty boots) and driving tractors pulling the trees from the apex to ensure it did not tumble on the visitors. Little did they know how much danger they were in. The summer weather was lovely and picnic lunches fun with most of the semi-literate juveniles spouting poorly comprehended philosophy and politics.

The longest and possibly most boring employment was six months at Barclays Bank between school and university. I was employed as a junior clerk through the usual route - nepotism. As very much a virgin I fell in love with all of the female staff and saved the money to enjoy my first holiday abroad by myself with Frank, Nick, and Stan to the glorious Lido at Jeselo. The waiters took the piss out of us, we enjoyed the speed and danger of 50cc mopeds but, joy of joy, I was the only one to 'score' – I was no longer uninitiated. I was in love – for 2 weeks at least. My dress sense was also validated because, much to my friends' amusement, I had bought a white imitation leather coat with large lapels. A sweet American couple stopped me in St Mark's square and asked where they could buy the coat for their son.

I loved cricket although I only ever made the school 2nd XI as a modest, medium paced seam bowler. As I hit my teens, I also played for Oatlands cricket club. At 16 I went to my first Test Match with my mate Frank at the Oval Test against the Aussies in 1968. I remember it clearly for many reasons and not only because Frank (or his dad) as a member and, therefore, whilst it rained, we drank quantities of beer in the members bar. My hero John Edrich had scored his usual nuggety century; followed by the South African born Asian cricketer Basil D'Oliveira scoring an exciting 150 odd runs. Cricket aficionados will remember this was the innings which finally forced the reluctant English cricket authorities to call him up for the tour of South Africa which, in turn, resulted in South African authorities calling off the tour.

Finally, we won the test with the crowds mopping up a soaking pitch which allowed Derek Underwood to 'mop up' the Aussie 'tail' and Frank and I mopped up the beer.

Playing in the match was Johnnie Gleesan as Australia's spinner, best known for his peculiar two fingered grip. Together with another couple of members of the Aussie team, he played in a show business match for charity, and I made up the numbers in one of the teams.

Tennis was my favourite non-team sport, and I was lucky enough to play at the lovely lakeside St Georges Tennis Club, amongst the St Georges celebrities which did not impress me because I had spent most of my life in close proximity to the stars of the day from Cliff Richard to Norman Wisdom. I attended an afternoon party at Norman's house in Pulborough, before he moved to the Isle of Man, where in a lovely swimming pool he indulged in acrobatic dives from the swimming board. However, at seven years old, I could do better and boasted that I had 4 diving boards – referring to the wooden corners on my 2ft deep 8ft x 8ft plastic paddling pool. I have always been full of bravado.

Schooling went smoothly with an acceptance at Lincoln College, Oxford. I suspect my college life differed very little from 80% of other students – the main object being to have a bloody good time and scrape a reasonable 2nd class degree. I succeeded in both those targets, even holding the record for the consumption of Newcastle Brown at the Lincoln College Boathouse, followed by being instrumental in capsizing the Third Lincoln Rowing Eight.

Chapter 5
My First Car
(The M.G. 1100)

My interest in the Motor Car continued but no car for me yet, although I passed my test within three weeks of my 17th birthday.

It was a learning process not without hazard, having backed my mother's car into a pub sign - an indication of problems to come. By 1969 she had replaced her Austin A35 with a **Riley Elf** in two tone Cotswold Blue and White. It was a delightful little car (until I got hold of it) being an up-market version of the Mini, extended by a tiny boot and filled with leather and wood. Its sibling, the **Wolsey Hornet**, was very similar but with a smaller oval wood dashboard.

The engine capacity never made 1000cc and then when, shortly after I passed my test, I discovered it did not have the power to run a set of roadworks resulting in a minor head-on collision - although not minor for the poor little Elf.

By 1969 Jaguar had introduced the **XJ6 series** with two engine sizes (2.8 and 4.2). Long wheel versions were introduced in 1972 and shortly afterwards the fabulous 5.3 V12 version. Dad, however, made his mind up early and stuck to it for many years, changing his **4.2 short wheelbase Jaguar** every two years for twelve years. The colours ranged from silver to yellow. On one of his 25 Long Playing Records ('John Hanson Sings Love Songs of Today') the cover photo captures Dad draped nonchalantly across the bonnet of his new silver, series XJ6.

I was into my second year at university and, after a year of bashing the Elf around, Dad decided I should have an old bomb to wreck. The funds available were limited but as I was the first in my 'gang' at Uni to own a car, I was more than happy. This was No.1 of 68. What could you buy for £200 in 1971? Well apparently, half an MG 1100. Do not get excited; this is not the MG sports car of either the minor or major variety. MG was part of the awful BMC (British Motor Corporation) later to become the even worse BMH, a merger with Jaguar in 1966 and finally to become the diabolical Leyland Motor Corporation in 1968

- an organisation noted for shop floor union activity and coincidentally shoddy workmanship. It became the ultimate example of failed socialist intervention in industry with the Labour Government's backing. It had more to do with the destruction of the motor industry in the UK than any other factor.

Even Jaguar quality suffered but fortunately Dad never purchased his cars long term. Later, as you will see, I made the mistake of buying cars of this era well after their sell-by-date. Typically, there was nothing wrong with the design concept of the 1100. It was a rebadging of the Austin and Morris 1100, a 'sportier' version. It was an attractive low-slung hatchback without the opening hatch. Cleverly, the engine was mounted transversely allowing a small car to offer a lot of interior space. It had a top speed of 88 mph and an engine producing 55 bhp.

It was the interior which sold it to Dad and me, being a clone of the Riley Elf interior with plenty of leather and wood. Exterior colour was British Racing Green with a grey interior in very good nick. Superficially it was a nice little car, a love of style over substance. The difficulties only became apparent when we took Mum for a first test run. Sitting in the back she marvelled at the luxurious comfort but questioned whether she should be able to see the road beneath her feet. A closer inspection revealed absolutely nothing - the rear floor pan had completely rusted away. To be fair to the purchasers, I was a naive 18-year-old and Dad, no engineer, was only used to buying new Jaguars from H.W. Motors, Walton-on-Thames. The car was taken off the road and finally we found a body shop which would weld it together - probably far stronger than the original manufacture. Fifty years on I remember the cost because it was exactly the same as the cost of the car - £200. For some reason I decided to remove the hubcaps and paint the wheels bright yellow!

For those parents of students for whom they have purchased a car whilst at university please skip to the end of this chapter. To sum up shortly, do not do it! The risk is obvious - your child becomes a taxi driver for a group of alcohol driven and reckless young people. It is highly unlikely that your progeny will take the 'vow' whilst undertaking the driving. I will not bore you with an undiluted review of the stupid and dangerous journeys I made with my mates in the next nine months. However, one of our regular pub haunts was the 'Trout' outside Oxford which frequently opened late back in the 1970s. This allowed me to drive back in a less than sober state. On one occasion I must have been worse than usual as I accepted a wager to drive back to Oxford on the wrong side of the road!

However, I finally got too ambitious, transporting five or six mates to London for a party in Kensington. Whilst enjoying ourselves we learnt of another party close by and the crowd piled into the 1100, together with a couple of extras. I remember clearly the police car sitting opposite us, a Morris Minor, but we completely ignored it. The engine started and just before I began to move there was a knock on the window and I was requested to disembark! After breathing into the bag, I was transported to the station and spent a few hours in the cell amenably discussing the party and my extraordinary consumption with my hosts.

Unfortunately, even if I had wanted, I could not hide my arrest from Mum and Dad because the press, latching onto the story, reported that Dad had been arrested and charged. The publicity machine had to rush into action requiring retractions! As my hearing was not listed for several months, I got on with life, including driving down to the West Country to join Dad whilst he was performing a summer season - he really was a most forgiving father. My first attempt at employment was as a deck chair attendant on Paignton beach. In a wonderfully egalitarian gesture, I was rejected by the Council because my hair was too long, despite my Oxford credentials.

Eventually, I was employed by Pontins Holiday Camp as one of the two male wine waiters serving four hundred campers with fifty waitresses – even I could find a girlfriend with those odds. Finally, I ended up as head wine water (the only wine waiter) at the Berry Head Hotel partly because it was hosting the mayor's late night dinner party for all of the showbiz stars appearing on the English Riviera (including Dad). No nepotism in the 1970s.

The end of August saw my starring role at the Bow Street Magistrates Court with no legal representation. This may have been a mistake as I pleaded guilty and then tried to plead in mitigation that my car had not moved and so the police had no right to breathalyse me. It wasn't a bad argument if I had not already pleaded 'guilty'. As expected, the verdict was a twelve month ban and a fine.

You would think my mates and I would have learnt our lesson. However, to 'celebrate' the ban, I jumped on the train to Chester, immediately after the verdict was given, to stay with Steve at his parents' home. His parents were conveniently absent. I will not recount the entire sordid tale, but it concluded by Steve driving his mother's car into a countryside ditch. We were collected by the father of one of the girls accompanying us and, in the circumstances, he was most understanding. He had two fine characteristics: first he was the owner and publican at one of Chester's finest countryside taverns and he drove a **Bristol 411!** A fine oddity of a car, still cherished by Bristol owners, it was an expensive hand-made sports saloon festooned with wood and leather, powered by the big Chrysler V8 engine with 6227cc. Twenty years later I visited Tony Crooks at the Kensington Showroom and almost bought one. I still haven't given up hope of making this final eccentric purchase. I think my recognition and appreciation of this rare vehicle helped to make up for putting his daughter in jeopardy.

So that was the end of the 1100 and driving for 12 months. This was somewhat inconvenient as my group of friends had decided to rent a cottage and converted stables in the country for our final year - naturally they had bought transport. We were fortunate, as students, to be accepted by the naive landlord as tenants. We hid behind a 'front', the accountant of one of our gang, Nitin. Nitin was the son of a millionaire industrialist from Uganda who was able to provide all of the referees and security. At the start of the term, Nitin borrowed a company Mercedes saloon until he was bought, one of my favourite small saloons, the **BMW 2002ti** in metallic blue. It started the BMW, and indeed modern, trend for fast, practical but sporty saloons. With the fuel injected engine, it was faster than the standard two litre engine and smoother than the Turbo version. I may have been a little jealous of the cars but not of the troubles that hit his family and business in Uganda with the arrival of the mad PresidentAmin. Coincidentally my future wife's family were also damaged as her uncle died in the 'the troubles' in Uganda and Colonel Gordon, her father, lost part of his savings having invested in his brother's Ugandan business. I became a hitchhiker and cadger of lifts for my last year, although it allowed me to focus on graduation.So, twelve months later, with a second-class degree from Oxford, I collected a late 21st birthday present - another car. After careful research we discovered that the only car for which I could buy insurance was **Volkswagen Beetle 1970.** To alleviate the embarrassment of driving a lawnmower, I chose one painted orange - as if that made it sportier. I know that there is a strong following for Beetles, and there have been modern versions of which I was later to become and owner, but the 1970 version was an awful drive - slow and very unstable at whatever speed one could achieve on a motorway. Still my lack of choice was entirely my own fault and at least this car had a sound body shell.

As it turned out it was only with me for six months. The plan had been for me to study at Chancery Lane College to pass my Part II Law exams and then attend my two-year articles (training contract) at a city law firm in February. However, the prospect of pin-striped suits, bowler hat and umbrellas appeared less and less attractive to a child of the stage. How could I postpone the inevitable? I would invent the twelve-month student break/sabbatical - a rare event in 1973/4.

So, much to my parents' disgust, I sold a stamp collection for £200 to Stanley Gibbons in the Strand (a not inconsiderable amount in 1974) and my unloved VW to fund my companion and I on a twelve-month break in Australia.

Chapter 6
Driving Australia in
a Ford Zodiac

The plan was to fly to Victoria and live for a short time with relatives of my companion in Geelong. It was a medium sized city sixty miles from Melbourne, and it was our intention to save some money and buy a car to tour the East Coast of Australia. I obtained a job as a barman for the cocktail bar at the only multi-story hotel in Geelong, the Travelodge. It was typically the Tri-Arc Travelodge design which had recently been completed and, with seven floors, was considered locally to be a skyscraper. It was a lovely cosy cocktail bar which kept open well into the early hours of the morning. In the 1960s the Australians had followed the American love of cocktails and I became a father confessor, at just 22, for many exhausted travelling salesman and women at 2am. Not a cocktail making expert, I borrowed a book and stuck to the recipes which inevitably recommended 2oz of each spirit and liquor. Naturally my cocktails were very popular, and it was only after the first monthly stocktake that I found out that the cocktails were priced on a 1oz measure. Fortunately, by then we were ready to move on, having purchased a very familiar vehicle - a *1957 Ford Zodiac Mark II*. It was the same model and colour, blue and white, of Dad's new version in 1957, just seventeen years on.

It was a steady vehicle and I decided to take it for a test drive along the gorgeous Great Ocean Road to Apollo Bay. The drive is spectacular for a traveller, with fabulous views of the cliffs, beaches, and ocean, although the Ford Zodiac was not best suited to the twisting road. A substantial queue built up behind us and I started counting the vehicles as they passed. This became a regular pastime on our future trip.

Stopping in Torquay (not Devon) at Bells Beach (a hardcore surfers' beach) we observed lithe young men performing foolhardy tricks on the waves; their panel wagons parked nearby, lined with carpet or velvet with attractive and adoring female acolytes decoratively draped across the bonnet. These days one would expect more female surfers and less disciples, but I suspect Australian beach culture is still very similar.

We drove on to Apollo Bay and on the return journey we stopped at the pretty seaside town of Lorne, and I made a left turn onto a 40 odd mile trip to Colac along a rough and partly made-up road. Colac was a small Victorian farming town, and the Shire clerk was the son-in-law of my hosts in Geelong. His duties focused on managing the municipality but in reality, they seemed to allow him ample time to partake in all sports proficiently (including Australian Rules Football, squash, tennis, golf) and shoot and fish the local wildlife to extinction. His poor wife was resigned to plucking and preparing dozens of wildfowl. However, one hobby which did interest me was his early love of Australian wine.

Until the 1960s beer consumption was the primary source of alcohol in Australia, supposedly limited by licensing laws which prevented the sale of alcohol after 06:00 p.m. As 06:00 p.m. beckoned the workers, who probably arrived at 05:00 p.m., lined up glasses and jugs of Australian lager and drank as much as possible before the pubs shut. This 'six-o'clock swill', as it was called, did not end until licensing laws extended hours in the 1960s. With the influence of the United States, cocktails became popular with the new middle classes, and, in my brief experience, they favoured the rich variety, such as Brandy Alexander with lots of cream.

Wine making had commenced by the mid-nineteenth century but had not really interested the average Australian until shortly before my arrival. South Australia was still the major wine producer and the prince of all wines, produced by Penfolds in the Barossa Valley, was the Grange Hermitage. It provided the entire Australian wine industry with credibility and was described as the most exotic concentrated Bordeaux (equivalent) in the world. Our hosts treated us to a variety of Australian Reds - primarily Shiraz and Cabernet Sauvignon grapes, all appearing divine to me. By late afternoon my host suggested I should join him and his mates for the Boxing Day Test when we returned from our travels, as England was touring Australia later in 1974 for the cricket Ashes.

Following my undertaking we set off on a journey of some 2400 miles from Melbourne to Cairns via the Coast Highway and taking in Victoria, New South Wales, and Queensland. A tough ask for a 17-year-old car but at 22, once we had bought some very basic camping gear, I was desperate to get in the old Ford and head North.

Chapter 7
Melbourne to Sydney

The old Ford chugged through the unattractive outer Suburbs of Melbourne as we hit the Princes Highway, set on reaching Lakes Entrance by evening. It sounded like an attractive destination, known for its 130 square miles of marshes, lakes, lagoons and ocean beaches with wonderful fishing and bird life. Lakes Entrance itself was a small tourist resort and adjacent to the famous 90 Mile Beach.

After about six hours of driving, we found it gloriously situated on a peninsula between two bodies of water - North Arm and Cunninghame Arm with a footbridge leading to the 90 Mile Beach. Our campsite was typical of many to come, namely government owned and situated by the water on the best block of land in the township. We erected the tent, and not having much experience, discovered that a two man tent is really a one-and-a-half-man tent - a tight squeeze.

We had learnt from our Geelong host that the best and cheapest way to eat in Australia was at the RSL clubs (Returned Service League). Australia, in the 1970s, took the support of their military veterans seriously with the RSL trying to provide the best possible support and services to all generations of veterans. This was largely funded by the RSL clubs which were found in almost every country town in Australia. The income was primarily created by gaming and alcohol. Australian's loved betting and it had a very egalitarian flavour with the pokie machines being a central part of most clubs. I always felt that when I found a club, I was in a proper Aussie town.

It is difficult to be censorious about the gambling because, as well as helping veterans, the RSL supported a variety of charities, including local sports, education, emergency services and aged care. The food was primarily sold at cost in large quantities and delicious. Frequently called Counter Teas (or Counter Lunches earlier in the day) but the meals had nothing to do with afternoon tea.

The customer ordered his or her generous protein dish, T-bone steak, fish, or shellfish, and then helped themselves from the counter selecting from a vast array of buffet style salads, with no limits on the number of repeat helpings. Even the beer and wine were very reasonably priced.

So, we filled up at the RSL that night and headed off the next morning on the Princes Highway to Sydney via Eden, Merimbula and Bega. Eden was a long redundant whaling station, with whaling banned in Australia after 1960. However, it was still a centre for whale watching and we hoped to catch a glimpse. We reached Eden after four hours and were staggered by the beauty of Twofold Bay, with Eden set on a peninsula splitting the bay in half. It still possessed a small harbour and a tuna fishing industry. In the 1970s the tuna canning factory was the town's major employer. However, like the Whaling, this was to disappear – this time due to the competition from the Thai factory fish industry.

One of the strangest marine stories in the region occurred without boats. The Yuin Tribe had availed themselves of the hunting prowess of the Orca or killer whale. The Orcas could herd the humpback whales into Twofold Bay and in trying to escape, they would beach themselves allowing the Yuin Tribe to harvest their meat and oil.

The spirits of the tribe's deceased inhabited the orcas and caused them to drive the whales, or so it was believed.

The landscape of the Sapphire Coast, as it was appropriately named, was blessed with long stretches of white sand beaches, with rivers blocked by sand dunes - hillocks created by waves and wind - resulting in vast lagoons of freshwater behind the beaches. 21 lakes in total often boasting pretty coastal townships such as Pambula, Merimbula, Tara Beach and Tathra. We had intended to stop the night but at a steady (queue creating) speed the Zodiac was holding out well, so we decided to chug towards Batemans Bay for a couple of hours. We did not possess the funds to enjoy Sydney, and this took us a bit closer to enable us, the following day, to circumvent it and find a campsite near the northern beaches. We were becoming spoilt, and Batemans Bay proved to be yet another picturesque coastal town. The names of the local hamlets are enough to paint a picture; Boathaven, Sunshine Bay, Surf Beach, Surfside, Hilli Pillli and others dotted around the splendid Batemans Bay and the Clyde River. Just after the bridge crossing the B-52 left the Princes Highway and headed off to the capital city Canberra. Better known as the Kings Highway, we hoped to follow this route on our return, although it was notorious as a death trap over the Clyde Mountain. We camped at a rough and ready site on the Clyde River and prepared for the long haul the following day. We were banking on about six to seven hours to reach our destination - Manly.

Again, the Zodiac had not let us down and within six hours we were crossing the Sydney Harbour Bridge (the 'Coathanger') and looking down on the Sydney Opera House by Circular Quay - two Aussie icons. The Opera House had been completed in 1973 after 14 years of construction. This was twice the time it took to build the Coathanger bridge forty years earlier. On the opposite Peninsula on the North Shore, stood Luna Park, a vast funfair constructed shortly after the bridge opened in 1935. By 1974 the park appeared somewhat shabby, facing the sparkling Opera House - the old and the new Sydney, the latter with its sophisticated pretensions. Luna Park went through a variety of owners, guises, and disasters, including an accident resulting in seven deaths in 1979. By contrast the Opera House became the architectural symbol of Australian success, despite the fact that the acoustics left much to be desired. They were so poor that the Opera House has had to shut to have AUS$150 million dollars spent on it. Comically, part of the problem was due to the Opera House not being large enough for classical operas!

I remember my dad frequently complained about modern theatres in the UK having poor acoustics, the star dressing rooms being miles away from the stage and in at least one nameless theatre, there was no access from one side of the stage to the other, requiring actors and singers to dash around the building exiting to the other side. Dad believed these absurdities were due to many modern Civic theatres being created by an unholy mix of architects and town councils who are largely ignorant of theatre and musical performance. Previously most theatres were capitalist ventures driven by show business, musicians, and theatrical managers. By the beginning of the twentieth century large private theatre chains had developed, such as Stoll and Moss with specialist theatre architects, for example Frank Matcham. After the Second World War funding changed with grants from the newly formed Arts Council and national and local government funding. In other words, control had moved away from the 'Business'.

We turned right off the Pacific Highway and left these icons behind and drove along the North Shore through Suburbs like Mossman, which all possessed delightful harbour ferry stations to take commuters and shoppers to Central Sydney. We continued over the bridge at the Spit, the earliest version dating back to 1928. Prior to its construction, Manly had really been a seaside resort rather than a Suburb of Sydney, despite the ferry links. As we approached Manly at close to 6pm, we could start to see why it was so geographically favoured. In front of us we could spy the ocean beach together with its pine trees whereas to the right we had caught a glimpse of Sydney Harbour and beaches together with a very substantial ferry terminal. It was clear from the map that the Suburb extended onto a national park and headland - the mouth of the harbour at the North Head.

We had decided to spoil ourselves that night and stay at the post-war 'splendour' of the Manly Hotel, built in a somewhat Aussie vernacular style. Sitting at the bottom of the parade, linking harbour to beach and opposite the ferry station, it seemed ideally situated for exploration the following morning. We woke up early and hit the main drag linking glittery harbour with surfing sea.

Manly's earlier status as a holiday resort meant the decaying remnants of seaside trivia suggested a connection with Margate rather than St Tropez. The same promise of seashells, jewellery of extravagant hues and candy floss made me feel in my comfort zone. This was partly because the southern UK seaside towns in Kent such as Margate, Ramsgate, Broadstairs and Deal were havens for retired show business girls and boys. The tacky seaside, sunshine (relatively speaking) and cheaper accommodation was a comfort to memories of wishful stardom. The real stars frequently hugged Surrey suburbs. Manly did possess some typically Aussie characteristics particularly the surf shops, great ice cream and coffee shops stemming from the recent settlement of Italian migrants. I found a fantastic example serving Italian croissants - heavy, cake-like, and sweet. I was used to the French variety with lots of butter, but this flowery and eggy Italian variety was superior in every way.

After a sunny picnic of cakes and coffee we decided to treat ourselves to an afternoon in Sydney City boarding a gracious old lady known as the Manly Ferry, which had the appearance of a paddle steamer without the paddles. The ferry chugged past multiple inlets housing impressive yachts. The fjord-like watery highway maximised the harbour views and dwellings clinging to the hillside. It took 30 minutes to reach Circular Quay proximate to the new Opera House and Sydney Harbour Bridge. Central Sydney did not match the glorious Suburbs in 1975; a large country town compared with London, but it was all to change in the future.

Chapter 8
A Dash to Cairns
and Back Again

The Zodiac was continuing to belie its years and we set off early the next day. Our intention had been to take in the North beach suburbs up to Pittwater and across to the Pacific highway but there appeared to be no link road, so we retraced our steps with the target of speeding up our trip. Our cash was dwindling and our transport slowing down.

Driving up the highway we passed Gosford and Woy Woy, Spike Milligan's (aka Terry) family home, where he was a regular visitor. When we had passed the coal capital, Newcastle, after about 4 hours, we were drawn to a road sign advertising 'Tea Gardens'. Unsure whether it was a catering establishment or a township we headed east towards Hawkes Bay. As we approached, we saw that this was another watery paradise with the meandering and wide Myall River lurching towards its estuary in the Tasman sea - across the river were its marine companions Hawkes Nest and Winda Woppa (yes this is a real mini township). We found a local campsite and on our journey up the main drag we noticed an attractive looking cafe called 'Tea for the Tillerman' and decided to stretch our funds that evening. Cat Stevens was at his peak and the LP, Tea for the Tillerman' had been a huge success five years earlier. It was something that we had not expected to find in the 'back of beyond'.

Some occasions linger in the mind after 45 years, perhaps because they are so unexpected and special. We consumed lovely local fish, fresh salads and drank fine New South Wales wine. The owner proved to be an architect having recently dropped out from Sydney and we drank into the early hours, at his expense, listening to Cat Stevens, Joni Mitchell, Carole King and all the current singer-songwriters. It summed up the 1970s for us and whilst writing this book I was delighted to see the cafe is still open serving good food, but I could never return. When a memory is that good you can never recreate it satisfactorily - the fact that it is now named 'The Tillerman', dispensing with the Cat Stevens connection, is a clear sign.

Two days later we had reached Queensland and in particular the Gold Coast. The Ford had passed through a series of holiday hotspots such as Port Macquarie and Coffs Harbour. In the 1970s however, it was Byron Bay which caught the eye. Again, a township punctuated by two glorious beaches divided by rocky headland and sitting on the north easterly point was Cape Byron lighthouse. In 1975 it was a charming but shabby beach village. It could not be really described as a holiday resort, rather a destination venue for surfies and sunshine dropouts. Shortly before our visit, the National Union of Students held a counter-cultural art and musical festival in Nimbin, near Byron. Many 'delegates' decided to stay, buy cheap land, and start up communes some were new age middle class looking for something different, others were vagrants, and some fell between the two categories. Sadly, Byron has been spoilt over the following decades with 'Sydneysiders' ploughing millions of dollars into holiday homes.

Our next stop was the Gold Coast and in particular Surfers Paradise, which was still a Paradise for surfers with only two tower blocks, the Apollo and the Illuca, a small network of canals and even some sand dunes still existing. Again, history suggests we were reaching all these coastal destinations before they fell afoul of their own success.

For now, we drove through, heading for the beach resorts north of Brisbane known by another unique name, the Sunshine Coast! We had been informed that Noosa Heads was the least developed with the added advantages of the Noosa River creating river beaches, Noosa beach, Noosa Headland, and Sunshine Beach on the other side of the National Park. Even in 1975 Hastings Street had a faint air of St Tropez sophistication and, let's face it, Australia in 1975 was not noted for its sophistication.

We found a tatty motel on the beach for a night of luxury before hitting the road - we could afford no more expensive stops if we wanted to reach Cairns. The Zodiac was beginning to show the effect of 1200 miles, overheating and I had doubts about the clutch which was squeaking when pressed. We still had another 930 miles and even averaging 50 mph it was 18 hours of driving. We decided to try and cover the ground in two days with one stop over. It was a shame because there were a lot of sights to see on the way up with the coast facing the Great Barrier Reef; it would have to wait for another trip.

To the east was Fraser Island, over 100km of sand and the largest sand island in the world. Next was Bundaberg - Rum capital of Australia, Rockhampton, Mackay, and Airlie Beach - the gateway to the Whitsunday Islands, a wonderful sailing mecca.

By this time the weather was becoming hotter and more humid as we headed north, well past the Tropic of Capricorn and into the tropics. Fields of sugarcane lined the road but our friend, the Ford, was beginning to become a serious issue. The gears were crashing, and we stopped every 50 miles to top up the coolant. We had reached the small country town, Bowen, and decided to have a rest at a small rocky cove deciding what to do next. It was still another 350 miles to Cairns; we were down to our last few dollars and our poor vehicle was in dire need of attention. Could we make it to Cairns but even if we could, what about employment? The alternative was Surfers Paradise where we had acquaintances and employment was plentiful. As we were pondering on our dilemma, laid out in the baking sun on the beach a horrible group of urchins marched around the beach sticking, under our noses, on a sharp stick what appeared to be a revolting stone. In fact, it was a stonefish. About 12 inches in size and described by our saviours as poisonous and deadly - both statements we found out later to be true. Now this had no tangible connection with our decision but when in doubt look for an Omen. For no particular reason we considered that this Omen dictated a rapid backward race to Surfers Paradise, covering about 600 miles. To provide some perspective we had already travelled the equivalent distance of London to Istanbul taking in Belgium, Germany, Austria, Hungary, Serbia, and Bulgaria. It was astonishing that our intrepid 17-year-old zodiac had lasted this long and yet we were asking it to travel the equivalent of London to Nice in two days or so.

As we hit our Surfers Paradise campsite our old friend literally crunched to a halt with steam pouring from the radiator, not to move again without help. We paid our campsite levy and there was not an Aussie dollar left for milk or bread. I was even tempted to ring for help from kind parents - something I vowed never to do.

I immediately rushed out to search for a part-time function waiting job over the weekend. Such jobs are readily available in a holiday hotspot and had two advantages they paid instant cash and double time on a Sunday. By Tuesday we were solvent after finding a job at the Surfers Paradise hotel - a lovely 1930s Building and the first hotel built by Jim Cavill in 1924 as he developed the entire Surfers Paradise site. The building was a brick replacement for its wooden predecessor burnt down in 1936 resulting in not only the residents being rescued but also the animals from the private Zoo. Lions and monkeys had roamed the streets for several days. A colourful history culminated in a sit-down strike by women customers refusing to move from the bar in a revolt against licensing laws which barred women drinking at the bar. By the time I started working there it was only 8 years before this bit of history was demolished - Surfers Paradise was never concerned with history.

Chapter 9
Surfers Paradise and
Beyond – A Rejuvenated
Zodiac

We decided to remain in Surfers for six months and repair the Zodiac and our finances. It was a touch tacky, but Surfers was always fun, warm, and sexy - it was becoming an anything goes destination, copying Miami. Following a week's employment, we could afford to repair the old lady and she returned to us, shining with a new clutch and radiator. The next task was to find some permanent accommodation. The canal development of the Nerang River behind Surfers had commenced. Surfers itself was set on a sand spit. The development allowed apartments and houses to have water frontages. By 2020, the Gold Coast boasted nine times more waterways than Venice. I couldn't afford the waterfront, but I could afford one of the older one-bedroom flats on Chevron Island. Surprisingly for Surfers it was not man-made, rather an existing island formerly known as Goat Island.

Prior to any major development, the area was a rather ramshackle but charming 'village', and, after the Second World War, several Hollywood movie stars visited including Laurence Olivier, Vivien Leigh, Lauren Bacall, and Katharine Hepburn. By the 1950s two colourful businessmen saw the potential and in different ways made their marks - Stanley Norman and Bernie Elsey.

Norman, through his corporate front, Chevron Holdings, focused on developing real estate including Chevron Island and the Surfers Paradise Hotel in which I worked. He was a Polish emigre, in love with Miami and for twenty years the prime mover until financial problems in the 1960s.

His main competition was an English immigrant Bernie Elsey, who arrived in Australia in 1915 at nine years old. Uneducated and a jobbing plumber, he was forty before he reached the wild frontier of Surfers. He quickly decided on a modus operandi for exploiting the area - sex. Surfers Paradise became the first Australian town to encourage bikinis and employed meter maids dressed in gold lame bikinis employed to fill expiring parking meters with coins, rather than booking visiting tourists. Their presence and website continue into the present day.

To create publicity Bernie held his famous pyjama parties at his private motel where many beautiful bodies ended up in the pool. Most parties were busted by the police and always ended up on the front pages - the primary purpose of the party. Hawaiian nights followed with grass skirts and not much else.

He tried to attract stars including the Beatles, but he changed his mind when they expected free food - was this the Beatles' inspiration for Rita the Meter Maid? He replaced them with the Gibbs Brothers - not yet the Bee Gees! So, the Beachcomber Motel, a very ordinary venue, with fairly tame parties, became the Sin City of Australia.

I never met Bernie although he was still around in 1975 but we got to know his ex-wife pretty well. She had the best stocked bar in Surfers, stock from Bernie's wholesale supply when they split up - some great parties were held. There must have been a touch of gypsy in her because when playing an early recording of J Cale, she prophesised that he would always be my favourite musician. It proved that I was in good company as he was also a favourite of Eric Clapton.

My new flat won no glamour awards, being typical of early Surfer's design - breezeblocks, tiled floors, black metal windows and doors with fly screens and a tired old air-conditioner. However, after five weeks in a one-and-a-half man tent it was five-star luxury.

I had now acquired a full-time job as a room service waiter but the hours and some of the requests were distinctly uncivilised and rather personal. So, I found a beachside restaurant and worked as a wine waiter. Whilst chatting with one customer he suggested that I could earn more working for him at a gravel pit site, ten miles inland. Nothing ventured, nothing gained; I had a go. However, I soon realised my new employment consisted of sitting on a heap of gravel, scorching in the sunshine, and ticking off the trucks. It soon became apparent my compatriots considered I was hired as a spy! Indeed, I discovered gravel had gone missing and leading to some aggressive confrontations - back to wine-waiting. It allowed freedom during the day to enjoy the sun, beaches, and trips to the interior countryside.

The Hinterland was rich with volcanic soil and filled with National Parks created by an ancient shield volcano resulting in the McPherson range. The landscape consisted of rugged cliffs, deep ravines filled with tropical rainforest, yet only thirty minutes from Surfers Paradise.

Mount Tamborine and our favourite area Springbrook, had fabulous views, waterfalls in abundance and luscious vegetation - a fairy land of different types of rainforests. Amazingly it contained four types - dry, subtropical, warm temperate and temperate. It was also full of wildlife including bird-of-paradise, bower birds, possums, marsupials, frogs, lizards, snakes (of course) and spiny crayfish.

Mount Springbrook was a fair height at 3100ft but most of the area was really a plateau known as the Switzerland of Queensland. We tried to escape from Surfers glitter most weeks and frequently stopped over for a coffee or lunch at the Springbrook Cafe. One day we decided to splash out and buy a bottle of wine with our beef burgers and salad. Reading the very short list, I was amazed to see a 1960s Penfold Grange Hermitage at a ridiculously low price - I suspected it had been on the list from the birth of a cafe. A lack of decanting tools and plastic cups rather detracted from our enjoyment, but a bargain is a bargain. We used our handkerchiefs to decant very badly and enjoyed our first taste of real luxury.

The end of the six months was almost over, far too quickly. However, we were tanned, fit, and funded; it was time to begin to return to Victoria and ultimately to the UK. I was committed to commencing my articles (training contract for solicitors) in February and before starting I had to pass two final exams - accounts and tax. My stay in Paradise was shortly ending.

Chapter 10
Farewell to Australia
and the Zodiac

Our travel plans consisted of driving back down the coast to Sydney and tracking inland to Canberra to visit the artificial capital – a city created for government because Sydney and Melbourne could not agree on which was kingpin.

As the centre of government, Melbourne had the prime claim, but Sydney was the older colony. Until Federation in 1901, each state governed separately under the Imperial Parliament in Britain, namely Victoria, Western Australia, Southern Australia (incorporating the Northern Territory), which supported Melbourne as the capital and Queensland and New South Wales supporting Sydney as the capital. Everyone seemed to ignore Tasmania! The Canberra area was chosen primarily for location rather than beauty. It was inland and southwest of Sydney at the foot of the Snowy Mountains (seven hours from Melbourne and four-and-a-half hours to Sydney). The area became the Australian Capital Territory and construction began in 1913 following a design competition was won by an American husband and wife team – the Griffins.

It took 80 or so years before all government agencies could be persuaded to move there – Canberra's attractions lagging a long way behind its sponsoring cities.

The lake, which was the focal point of the original design, did not get built until the 1960s (Lake Burley Griffin) and even then, it took over a year to fill due to a local drought. Nothing seems to happen quickly in Canberra, not apparently engendering any great affection in the Australian psyche despite recent claims it is the best city in the world to inhabit. Boiling summers, cold winters, isolated and without great cultural significance, even Australians must doubt that claim. It took 60 years to replace the provisional Parliament Building – say no more.

The journey was long but uneventful as we headed into town along wide boulevards and passing what seemed to be the University and main residential area. Then across the bridge, over Lake Burley Griffin, into the administrative, political, and diplomatic hub. The Old Parliament building to the east together with a multitude of National Galleries, museums, convention centres and embassies. Despite these architectural highlights, the area seemed like a quiet and attractive country town more than a capital city.

Therefore, once we had scooted around the major attractions, we determined to leave this artifice and return to normality by heading towards the Snowy Mountain range. It was a long-held ambition of mine to visit the area made famous by the wonderful Banjo Paterson, a poet who managed to conjure up the essence of Australia at the time of the Federation. A rugged satirical commentary of the outback and country folk in poems like 'Man from Snowy River', 'Clancy of the Overflow', the 'Man from Ironbank' and of course, the real Australian national anthem, 'Waltzing Matilda'. My personal favourite, however, had to be Johnson's Snakebite Antidote. It starts:

> *Down along the Snakebite River, where the overlanders camp,*
> *Where the serpents are in millions, all of the deadliest stamp;*
> *Where the station-cook in terror, nearly every time he bakes,*
> *Mixes up among the doughboys half-a-dozen poison-snakes:*
> *Where the wily free selector walks in armour-plated pants,*
> *And defies the stings of scorpions, and the bites of bull-dog ants:*
> *Where the adder and the viper tear each other by the throat,*
> *There it was that William Johnson sought his snake-bite antidote.*

Seven verses later, he, of course, almost dies of his own concoction.

We had decided to see as much of the Snowy region as possible, even though there was very little snow left. So, we headed down the Monaro Highway to Cooma and West through to Thredbo and Perisher, primarily ski resorts of the Kosciuszko National Park – Kosciuszko Mountain the tallest peak in Australia at 7,310ft. With no skiing and the countryside, lovely, but starting to burn bronze the area it was not at its best. We stayed the night at Thredbo and wished we had not because whilst parking, we, rather unfortunately, backed up into an animal which must have limped off. We went searching for it but to no avail – the reception suspected that it may have been a wombat common in those parts. We were told they had the appearance of mini bears but were inquisitive, stubborn and could attack if approached. So, despite our concern, we may have been lucky not to have found the victim.

The next day we completed the three-quarter loop through Khancoban (a pretty village) and via the Snowy Valleys Way to wine growing Tumbarumba and finally up to Tumut. The scenery was picturesque with plains and valleys surrounded with mountain Peaks.

From Tumut, we decided to attempt the direct route to Melbourne along the inland Hume Highway. Normally a six-hour drive but in our ancient Zodiac, it was 12 hours or more by the time we reached our host in Geelong who had offered to put us up for another month until we returned to the UK. Much of that month was to be spent by me studying for the two extra exams, whilst soaking up the hot summer sun in the back garden.

We were sad to say goodbye to our brave and steadfast friend but after driving for 4000 miles (or about half the distance back to London), we recovered the full cost of the Zodiac plus a little extra – the advantage of the purchase of a car rather than renting one. However, before we said goodbye, I had an Ashes engagement with my Colac mates. The English cricket team was visiting the Aussie shores for the Ashes, and, to date, it had not achieved much success. During the first two tests in Brisbane and Perth, they had been verbally and physically abused. It was the Lillee and Thompson era – a fearsome fast bowling duo. The Aussie team was depicted as the 'ugly Australians' (by the 'poms' at least) and Wisden, the cricketing Almanac, stated that 'never in the 98 years of test cricket have batsmen been so grievously battered by ferocious, hostile short, pitched balls'. This was, of course, before the West Indies teams followed.

After the Brisbane test, so many batsmen were injured that the selectors invited poor Colin Cowdrey to join the team at the age of 41 years old; a fine batsman but well past his best. As a gentleman, he greeted his tormentor, Jeff Thompson, courteously only to receive the response 'that's not going to help your fatso – piss off'. Later Thompson boasted, "Truthfully, I enjoy hitting a batsman more than getting him out. It doesn't worry me in the least to see the batsman hurt, rolling around screaming and blood on the pitch." An honest man or perhaps, he was just a charmless thug let loose with a lethal weapon.

As usual the Australian media and crowds took their lead from their team abused the English Team. The umpires refused to enforce law 46 which prohibited continuous short pitches and intimidating bowling, fearing a booze-soaked Australian crowd invading the arena and throwing even more beer cans. It was to this gladiatorial encounter that I was invited in that vast arena of the Melbourne Cricket Ground for the Boxing Day test. This was the Australian cricket mecca, seating 70,000 or 80,000 Australian parochial supporters. This was before the 'barmy army' (the overseas English supporters club) was developed to provide a barrier to the local aggression. Our host and three of his Aussie Rules mates planned to drive to Geelong and switch to the Zodiac for the next 50 miles taking us to the MCC. I was informed they would have one or two tinnies at the ground and, in return for my ticket, I was to stay relatively dry and chauffeur them back to Geelong where they considered the journey back to Colac less legally hazardous.

Therefore, on the 26th of December 1974, four very tall men, aged 25 to 30, climbed into the Zodiac. As none of us had taken any interest in the news, we had no idea that in the early morning of Christmas Day Father Christmas had provided Darwin, the capital of the Northern Territory, with an extra present – Cyclone Tracy, which destroyed the small city. Later, it was to play a big part in my life.

It was only when we arrived at the MCC that I realised how enormous this Aussie Rules football stadium appeared against the horizon. Many of the spectators were already the worse for wear. On the journey to the ground, I had been asked by my passengers to stop at a drive-in bottle shop to fill four very substantial eskies. We parked the Zodiac and found our way to the front of the spectator enclosure. Behaviour was relatively controlled in the morning amongst the spectators but very fiery on the field where the English batsmen were peppered with short, pitched bowling. Goodness, batting progress was slow, only 40 runs for the loss of 2 wickets in the morning and in the afternoon, 76 runs were scored by Cowdray and Edrich. Both were hit several times, and both dismissed in a highly unfortunate manner. First Cowdrey, after he lost concentration following a spectacular pitch invasion and Edrich to a highly dubious caught behind umpiring decision.

After the break for tea, the now stupendously drunk crowd, including my new friends, were very bored and looking for any entertainment. As Frank Tyson noted (the former English fast bowler), 'crowd behaviour had deteriorated with exhibitionists in a drunken stupor invading the pitch'. Perhaps as a masochistic gesture, to provide an alternative source of entertainment, my so-called friends grabbed me and lifted me higher in the air shouting 'this guy's a bloody Pom'.

Thereafter, showers of beer cans rained down upon us. Fortunately, most missed, hitting our neighbours and resulting in general warfare, rather than a particular focus on me.

After Tony Grieg had been dubiously run out, an umpiring decision probably influenced by the crowd behaviour, England crumbled to 177 for 7 wickets in a day's cricket. Actually, this go-slow worked and four days later, England were able to draw the match, although Australia was to win the next two matches. Fortunately for England this was a six-match series and the England captain Mike Denness, who had earlier dropped himself, scored a massive 188 allowing an England innings win; too little too late.

Chapter 11
A Glamorous Return but No Motor Cars!

We were reluctant to return to a grey February in England, still recovering from strikes and three-day weeks. By this time, the precursor to Brexit had taken place, namely joining the European community in 1973. As always, it had caused complex debate in the nation – dividing the Labour and the Tory Parties. The unpopular Heath Tory government had been beaten by Labour, led by an unwell Harold Wilson, who only had a minority in Parliament. The country was to have a chance to vote in a referendum as to whether the UK should withdraw only two years after joining!

This was to await us. Shortly before I returned, I received a phone call from the ITV asking whether they could fly us home from Australia first class because John Hanson Senior was to be the surprise guest on 'This is Your Life', to be hosted on television on the 12th of February 1975. Dad was at the peak of his career having staged a series of successful revivals in the West End of London, including the ubiquitous Desert Song and the Student Prince, and was shortly to produce a gold record Award for his K-Tel LP.

The show had a set format in which Eamonn Andrews (charming Irish host) would invite the celebrity to a decoy location, present him with a large red book with a personal history and then taken back to a studio with an audience and invited guests – John Hanson: 'This Is Your Life'.

Well, I was delighted (despite already owning a return economy ticket) because from our first-class airline seats we were to be taxied to our good quality Hampstead hotel where we were to imbibe and eat courtesy of the ITV. I was still revising for my exams and indeed, I had to take them whilst staying at the hotel – all we had to do was hide from Mum and Dad. I obtained a liking for Bollinger champagne, smoked salmon, and scampi Provençale.

After the show and our fabulous last-minute appearance stealing the show of course, there was a party at which guests were handed very generous packets of cash for expenses.

It was now time to knuckle down for two years to complete my training and I had chosen, or rather I had been chosen by a city firm, now-defunct, Herbert Oppenheimer, Nathan and Vandyk. I had chosen to rent one of the first flats in the Barbican. As it was located only ten minutes' walk away, there was little excuse for a car, sadly.

The development showed its 1960s origins constructed from reinforced concrete, with both tower block and low-rise housing included. Noted for long corridors, it resembled scenes from Orwell's '1984'. It surrounded and dominated the mediaeval St Giles Cripplegate Church. The huge project was unfinished as I occupied my split level one bedroom flat in Ben Jonson House and of course, the cultural additions, such as the concert hall, theatre, galleries, and cinemas were the last to be added. Nevertheless, it was a pretty cool pad for a 23-year-old articled clerk earning £2,500 a year! However, no cash for a motor car.

My own life, to date, had been split – term time with school and suburban and holidays following Dad around the country like gypsies, although his revivals in London had meant some home comforts. However, it did not equip me for the City of London work life in the mid-1970s. The principal solicitor to whom I was articled, wore pinstriped suits, a bowler hat and carried a rolled-up umbrella. In contrast, I was used to mid-morning socials at the Kardomah cafe with the chorus and late evening meals at the local theatrical bistro. Of course, not all lawyers followed this conservative style and the closer you get to the West End, the more flamboyant the dress sense – 'the velvet jacket brigade'. My own preference was 1930s Chicago, with pinstripe black suit and white tie. This was muchto the disgust of my mentor whose supervision consisted of taking me out to lunch at one of his many London clubs. Friday nights were special as I was usually performing at small restaurants with my passible voice and lousy guitar accompaniment. I would stroll down the huge Victorian staircase dressed in denim with my acoustic guitar by my side – a provocative but childish gesture!

Clearly, I had no intention of remaining with the firm when I qualified. Much of my time was spent at that Victorian obsession with the neo gothic, namely the Law Courts on the Strand. I gradually learned to navigate my way through the labyrinth of corridors, frequently terminating in cul-de-sacs from poor planning and interminable extensions. Much of my time was spent in the 'Bear Garden' which had nothing to do with bears but something to do with baiting – baiting articled clerks. In my initiation, I lined up with other novices to be chewed up by quasi judges known as Masters. They dealt with litigation procedural matters and, as apparent bitter old men, enjoyed humiliating the new boys. In fact, it worried me not a jot and, after a few enjoyable skirmishes, these geriatric bullies looked for easier targets.

My sight was clearly focused on a return to Australia, although my determination briefly wavered when I was approached by Brian Eagles, the head of the entertainment law department. His practice was unusual because most show business stars prefer to be closer to the West End – close to Bond Street and Mayfair. However, he attracted a good client base by tending to all of their everyday needs – pampered, which included their pets.

Just before my articles ended, Brian offered me a position as a 'legal nanny' because he assumed that my show business background would enable me to deal with these pampered pooches. However, 25 years of intimate knowledge of extravagant egos (my father being least guilty) made the offer unattractive and so, as my employment terminated, I made plans to return to Australia. The only useful gesture made by my principal partner (Nathan Jr) in my two years at the firm was to provide me with reference to a family connection in Sydney at Freehill, Hollingdale and Page.

However, as usual, I decided to take a more difficult route via Perth.

Chapter 12
A Return to Australia –
The Morris Marina

The attraction of Perth as a destination (rather than Sydney) was that it was possible in 1977 to fly to Singapore and hop on a livestock carrying vessel to Perth. The cost was no more than flying the whole way; we did not expect expat luxury and we did not get it. As we boarded the vessel in Singapore, there was a distinct animal smell, although the livestock transport was normally one-way – Perth to Singapore; humans deposited, and livestock collected (and some passengers as well).

From memory, the vessel was called the Kota Sinapura or similar, which was apparently scrapped a few years later. The cabin was full of brown teak and very basic bunk beds with a distinct rush of scurrying as we put on the light. Further investigation revealed cockroaches, presumably migrating from the lower livestock decks. We retired swiftly to the passenger deck and to the open-air bar. The weather was balmy, and the Aussie beer was duty-free. Apart from changing, showering, and eating, that is where we spent seven days; laid out on cane furniture, sipping tinnies and making acquaintances. We enjoyed glorious calm seas as we passed through the verdant islands of Indonesia. The dining hall resembled a second-rate public school, as did the food – mixed with oriental spices and served by a variety of nationalities (Malay, Filipino, Indian and others) but all very friendly.

As we sailed into Freemantle, Perth's port, a couple of our recent drinking partners asked whether we would like to share accommodation when we had found employment. First, we needed to move back into the car owning fraternity and, almost upon disembarking, we found our way to the used car dealers. I do not know why I did it. I cannot remember and I am not sure, if questioned, that I had any good reason for buying the *Morris Marina*. I now read that it is high on the list of the 'worst ever cars'. Perhaps it had something to do with enjoying one of the shortest development periods of only 18 months. Also, the build quality was instantly in doubt as soon as the name 'British Leyland was mentioned.

It was blessed with an ancient suspension, converted from the old Morris Minor and the wrong front suspension fitted in the production line. This resulted in understeer and bump steer on rough roads – just what you want in Australia. It was ugly and the colour was a horrible harvest gold (it reminded me of some bad curries). I suppose, in defence of my sanity, it was a relatively cheap car for four years old and low mileage. However, in all honesty, I think it was probably because I 'fell' in love with the after-sales mag wheels, a feeble attempt at sportiness. I am now amazed to discover it was a popular and successful model – I despair at the taste of car buyers in the 1970s. Perhaps it is made more understandable when one considers that the Marina's sister was the Austin Allegro which is also an ugly duckling on the list of 'worst cars ever'.

With the typical confidence of a 25-year-old, I walked off the street into the best firm in Perth asking for a job and was lucky enough to land one in the litigation department, starting immediately. I have always believed that being lucky enough to be in the right place at the right time is critical but, of even greater importance, is the ability to recognise that moment of fortune.

With a car and employment settled, we were able to rent a flat with our new friends 10 miles out of Perth at Scarborough. It was a small seaside village blessed with a glorious beach, and with the apartment on the edge of the dunes.

The law firm was full of good lawyers, with a large influx of South African lawyers at a time when the legal training in South Africa was the best in the world. In particular one ex-barrister was so good as to be obviously a future Chief Justice (which he became). I still had itchy feet and, although Perth was pleasant, it was very much a country town in 1977 – a comfortable town perched on the Swan River. We described it as 'Perfect Pink Perth' with the lovely hot sunsets.

After six months I was searching the 'Australian' for vacancies on the legal page. In infinite wisdom I decided to ignore an introduction to one of the best firms in Sydney and considered an advertisement where the job was outlined in limited detail, as was the description of the firm. However, I latched on to the fact that it was located opposite the beach in Maroochydore on the Sunshine Coast. Now, to the uninitiated, he or she may not realise that to accept this appointment I was required to drive 2800 miles, across the sun scorched Nullarbor ('no trees') plain, in a two-wheel drive rubbish vehicle. This decision was based upon a single two hour telecom! One might suspect the physical challenge was the real reason for the change rather than career progress.

I had clearly adopted the 'Old Australian Way' as described by Banjo Paterson:

'The narrow ways of English folk
Are not for such as we.
They bear the long-accustomed yoke
Of staid conservancy.
But all our roads are new and strange,
And through our blood there runs
The vagabonding love of change
That drove us westward of the range
And westward of the suns.'

In some ways we were lucky because the Eyre highway, which links Western Australia to South Australia, was only just finished as a bitumen covered road in 1976. An almost impossible track had existed for 100 years but only in the Second World War was the route, of some 1000 miles, improved to a rough track. It then took another 40 years before it was finally sealed.

I saw myself as an adventurer and I loved driving into unknown locations. I would have been more suited to being employed as a tea plantation manager 40 years earlier rather than as a lawyer. I suppose I didn't really want to work at all – certainly nothing permanent – six months was enough to top up our funds.

Chapter 13
Perth to Maroochydore –
The Morris Marina

I never seemed to leave enough time to explore properly. I also never had enough money to buy a decent vehicle and I always made the drive longer than I needed. On this occasion, we decided to go through Geelong again, adding another 450 miles onto the journey making a grand total of 3250 miles in three weeks and in a Morris Marina. It was 250 miles further than London to Jordan.

I allowed myself five days, staying at roadhouses, to reach Geelong – about 300–465 miles per day. The stopovers were to be Norseman, Eucla, Ceduna and Adelaide. If we were making good progress, an extra couple of nights in Adelaide was a possibility. Again, we were missing many sights along the way which was a shame as it was hardly a trip, I was likely to repeat. We did not even have time to explore the gold mining town of Kalgoorlie, although I was determined we would take a short detour so that we could at least have lunch there.

Kalgoorlie and Norseman proved to be disappointing – both owing their existence to gold mining, although Kalgoorlie was far larger and still remained a gold and nickel mining location. Kalgoorlie did boast some 'over the top' colonial Victorian architecture. This included the Exchange Hotel which was decorated with the typical metal roof verandas and provided a decent counter lunch.

The rest of the trip to Adelaide went by in a haze of dust and scorching sun. The road followed much of the Southern extremity so midsummer temperatures were not as high as expected but 35 degrees centigrade was high enough without air conditioning.

The Australian Leyland Marina had appalling suspension made even worse by the oversized tires and mag wheels. However, I was gratified to discover that the Marina had a bit of 'oomph' because, to compete with local competition, this vehicle was powered by the 2600cc six-cylinder engine and able to hit 60 miles per hour in less than nine seconds – not bad in 1977.

Therefore, with some discomfort, we discovered that although Nullarbor did mean 'no trees' in Latin, the main scenery was bluebush and scrub rather than sand as it was south of the Gibson Desert. It was necessary to be alert for wandering wildlife including kangaroos, emus and imported camels (left to become wild by earlier explorers and workers).

The early part of the Eyre highway, before the Nullarbor, was of more interest including the Fraser Range and the Dundas Nature Reserve. Parts of the highway were artificially created so as to avoid long passages of straight roads (for safety reasons), other than the 90 Mile Straight, which was one of the longest stretches of straight road in the world. We had no time to detour to go whale watching off the southern coast and, in our ignorance, we passed the Maralinga nuclear 'testing' ground 300 miles to the North.

Between 1956 and 1960, 312 nuclear explosives were detonated from the land and air. Many of the service personnel were permanently disabled and killed by the effects of the radiation. The local indigenous people were severely affected by the explosions and radiation, despite the Australian and British government continuing to deny their existence at the location. Later, public enquiries found that Prime Minister Menzies (an anglophile and snob) had misled the nation and his own government as to the dangers. Much of this has recently been publicised in in the film 'Operation Buffalo'.However, we were unaware of our proximity to this political embarrassment. The Marina had not won our affection but generally behaved well until we commenced the last leg of our crossing – Adelaide to Geelong. Just 50 miles from Geelong, the car was starting to smell decidedly oily, and we stopped in Ballarat, a gold mining centre filled with fine Victoriana created during the nineteenth century Gold Rush. Before we could disembark and enjoy it, flames issued from the engine bay. Fortunately, we had parked outside of a Victorian fire station and several firefighters rushed out and extinguished it rapidly. Clearly, 2000 miles in five days was too much for the poor Marina. The fire station was very grand with a fine four-story viewing tower and we were told by our saviours that it was the oldest continuously operating fire station in Australia. It was just another example of how important it is to have a modicum of luck.

As it was, the car was salvageable and when we reached Geelong, I arranged for it to be transported to a garage near us to be repaired. This was an unexpected cost and so our finances were draining fast – I needed employment soon! By visiting the garage every day, the Marina was repaired in four days and we were able to head off on our journey to Maroochydore via the Hume Highway.

Our target mileage was 400 to 500 miles a day – a distance of 1200 miles in total. The landscape was pleasant in Victoria as we passed through the Great Dividing Range (hills rather than crags). There was some eucalyptus forest but much of the countryside was farmland – including wine growing.

Without any motoring problems, we kept to our tight schedule and hit Maroochydore after three days. I'm not sure what I expected but in 1975, the Sunshine Coast, of which Maroochydore was a small part, was no better or worse than a dozen other underdeveloped east coast seaside holiday destinations. We drove up to the law firm in which I was intending to waste a fine legal education and it consisted of a single storey wooden building on the seafront (the good part). I had worked in first class law firms – I just could not see myself undertaking conveyancing and matrimonial work even if I could enjoy the ocean.

What should I do? I am embarrassed to reveal that I went to the closest telephone box, rang the firm and pleaded sickness; therefore, making it impossible for me to attend. I have never felt such a bastard, but I knew the work relationship would have been hopeless. I discovered I was a 'legal snob'. However, I was now unemployed with limited funds. Yet again, it required a dash down the coast to the Gold Coast and Surfers Paradise – at least, it was only a journey of four hours. This time, it was not as easy to pick up casual labour, as a lawyer. We stayed with our friend in Surfers whilst I looked for a temporary legal job in between catching up with JJ Cale. It is easy to see where my heart lay by recalling my favourite song, 'Call Me the Breeze':

Call me the breeze
I keep blowing down the road...
I ain't got me nobody
I don't carry me no load.

These were the aspirations of a 25-year-old which I'm afraid only lasted a few years when, like most people, I gathered dependents, debts, and possessions, but when it all became too much, I felt OK after a dose of J.J. who really lived up to his mantra. For much of his life, he lived in a mobile home, made a successful LP, and went missing whilst living on the proceeds. Eventually, my dreams were realised when I saw him at the Hammersmith Odeon where he looked distinctly uncomfortable – my companion thought he was one of the stagehands. Make no mistake, the guitar playing was magical.

My doorstep visits to Surfers lawyers, mainly conveyancers in this local property boom, resulted in a part-time paralegal job sorting documents for litigation – boring, boring, boring! This was never going to be a long-term appointment, which suited me!

Chapter 14
The Northern Territory –
Car Starvation

As luck would have it, a constant factor in a lucky life, I was perusing the Australian Newspaper legal pages and read an employment advert for a job in Darwin. I had no idea where Darwin was located but the name did ring a bell, although the events of Christmas 1974 were still a blank to me. I had a quick peek at a map and found Darwin located on a peninsula right in the middle of Australia in a quasi-state called the Northern Territory, of which it was the capital. It appeared to be closer to Denpasar than Sydney. If the internet had existed, by this stage, cyclone warning lights would have flashed. As it was, I went to the interview uninformed.

The luckiest part of the luck was that the interview was to be held at a hotel by a swimming pool on the Gold Coast! To a legal risk taker, the job had all the characteristics I was looking for, the absolute opposite of the City of London or indeed, Sydney lifestyle, an almost unbearable climate, a cornucopia of deadly wildlife (from 24ft saltwater crocodiles to poisonous snakes and insects) and in the middle of nowhere. I had no doubt that I would be the only Oxford/City trained lawyer in the Northern Territory in 1977 and, as far as I'm aware, I was right.

When I arrived at the hotel, I was invited by the receptionist to go out to the pool to find my interrogator. However, it was perhaps overstating the meeting to call it an interrogation – perhaps a sort of pleading. He was an impressive Australian – stocky and about 5 foot 6 inches with broad shoulders. He boasted a mop of brown hair and mischievous eyes – wearing tight long shorts, long socks and a Hawaiian shirt and proffering a can of Fosters.

He painted a picture of sandy beaches and sunshine. The job appeared to be a self-sustaining litigation practice and I was to receive half the profits after the deduction of overheads. There were no guarantees and therefore, I could earn a pittance but on the other hand, if successful, I would earn four times my previous salary in Perth. This was a financial adventure as apparently the current incumbent had moved to the independent bar.

In England, in 1977, there was a strict division between solicitors and barristers ensuring only the older profession (barristers) were allowed the right of audience in higher courts. This monopoly ensured that the judiciary was made up of ex-barristers. However, through partnership and corporation, solicitors now far outnumbered barristers and had assumed the mantle of real power in the legal world. This was not acknowledged by barristers, whose mantle of superiority really pissed me off.

However, it was explained to me that no such division existed in the Northern Territory, which was empowered to make its own laws (ordinances) and regulations. All legal practitioners have equal rights although, in a pale imitation of the English system, some practitioners had set themselves up as specialist advocates at a 'bar' to which my predecessor had attached himself.

Therefore, instead of being the older profession, the bar in Darwin was the younger profession. It would mean a step-up in advocacy status because until now, my appearances in courts had been limited to procedural work, not leading evidence, and cross-examination. This was not enough to deter me and when my inquisitor informed me that he had started the first legal practice in Darwin which was not government-sponsored in 1954, I warmed to him and the potential for a new adventure. There was a mention of a cyclone but by this time, I had talked myself into acceptance providing it was understood the contract was limited to 18 months.

It was time to sell the Marina and, when all was said and done, it had survived pretty well despite my misgivings. However, the sale did not bring tears to my eyes.

It is fair to say that my current companion was not enthusiastic, hence the contract was limited by time so that we could save money to return to the UK. A motor vehicle was not allowed by her. After our first 24-hours in Darwin, I could understand some of her reluctance. We arrived in the monsoon season – temperature in the mid-30s (centigrade), humidity 80% or more, thunderous rain and lightning strikes. We were buffeted into Darwin by the weather and eventually strolled from the plane, down the stairs into a damp inferno.

We searched for an air-conditioned terminal only to find Darwin International Airport consisted of a converted aircraft hangar with overhead fans.

Perspiring profusely, we were greeted by a tall and slender young man apparently sent to collect us by my employer. An interstate lawyer from Sydney, he led us to a shabby green VW and proceeded over the next 30 minutes to explain the attractions that Darwin offered.

The first characteristic which was patently obvious to the eye, was that Darwin was barely half built and lacking in any luscious tropical vegetation. I now learnt that two years earlier, Cyclone Tracey had wiped out the city, destroying most of the first floors of the tropical style housing leaving the stilts and not much else. It also killed over 60 people and the rest of the 46,000 people had evacuated. Apparently, some of the evacuees were returning to rebuild Darwin and I had been employed to help this process – this was news to me!

We then received an in-depth analysis of the climate – apparently, the monsoon season was not the least hospitable. Prior to the monsoon, rain will not have fallen for nine months and the humidity build-up after the 'Dry Season' and the unbearable heat resulted in what was known as the 'suicide season' – for obvious reasons. Fortunately, there were few skyscrapers (less after the cyclone) for sufferers to use as platforms. The one bright spot seemed to be the Dry Season which boasted three months of low humidity and cool temperatures (31 degrees centigrade). He did try and persuade us that, in fact, the monsoons were not too bad. The rains reduced humidity and the lightning strikes over the Timor Sea were stunning.

Finally, our narrator moved onto the dangerous wildlife. We were informed that the sea was unusable for most of the year. It was not so much the sharks and saltwater crocodiles but the 'stingers' - a vicious and deadly jellyfish which inhabited the water all year with the exception of the 'Dry Season'. He did not mention the poisonous spiders but did let slip that the Territory counted seven out of the 10 most deadly snakes in the world as part of its wildlife. He also failed to refer to the imported dangers such as huge water buffalo and feral pigs.

My reluctant companion vowed never to step outside off bitumen which, with the rains, was in any event impossible because of the bush roads being flooded – Darwin was an island until the 'Dry'. We were delivered to one of the few structures still intact because it was constructed of concrete – the Seaview Hotel in Fannie Bay. It sat opposite rough common land next to the Darwin Sailing Club, which we were informed was the focal point for all social life in Darwin, particularly following the cyclone. Sadly, it was a sailing club with very few boats after the cyclone and those that survived were not at sea during the monsoon.

Joy of joy, our hotel was air-conditioned, and we gradually cooled ourselves down. There was an unexpected visit from two tree frogs in our toilet. It placed us in a bit of a quandary as to where we were to relieve ourselves.

Chapter 15
The Virgin Advocate

I was to be admitted as a full-fledged barrister/solicitor or legal practitioner – the admission ceremony was something of a farce. I was forced to borrow the kit from one of my colleagues, including gown, shirt, bib, and wig - yes it was 35 degrees centigrade (outside the courthouse) and I still had to wear a wig. This proved to be tricky because it was at least three sizes too small. Therefore, as I was being proposed by my 'moving' advocate, I bowed to the presiding judge and the bloody thing fell off. Perspiring profusely (from embarrassment as the courtroom was an air-conditioned 5 degrees), I apologised, ground the wig back on my head at a jaunty angle and received a less than amused response from the Judge. He hardly gave me an unequivocal vote of approval: "Well Mr Hanson, I have been disappointed, nay horrified, by some of the standards shown by Counsel in this backwater of the Common Law legal world. However, I had blamed this slip shod practices on the old timers left to their own devices. Now, I must change my opinion and accept they are common to the recently admitted too."

However, I was now an admitted member of the profession and the next afternoon, I was asked to appear before the Federal Court. The Northern Territory did not have full State status and its appeal process was initially to a three judge Federal Court travelling from Canberra. Therefore, my first appearance was in front of the equivalent of the Court of Appeal. I was assured that it was an appeal by consent and that my predecessor, acting for the Appellant, had all the necessary information. I gathered the real reason for the appeal was that the Chief Justice had fallen asleep in the afternoon whilst presiding. I was also told not to mention it because judges do not like criticism of other judges.

By the time we had waited for the bottom of the list, I was very nervous indeed. My opponent proposed to the court that the appeal was agreed to by the respondents (me). The Chief Justice fixed his beady eyes on me and asked me to explain why the respondent 'agreed' to a motion which effectively meant the judge had made a mistake. Panicking, I mentioned the post luncheon judicial nap and my inquisitor was not best pleased. We were sent away to obtain more information.

I was also searching for accommodation which matched the limited budget imposed by my companion and within walking distance of the office. I had inspected a studio flat consisting of a space which had been enclosed under a typical Darwin house perched on stilts – one that had survived the cyclone. It was owned by a notorious chef in Darwin, notorious for excellent food and a foul temper in the kitchen. He was an exuberant leader of the gay community. 1977 was not noted for its open attitude towards the homosexual community but Darwin was different and so was I. A majority of the chorus line in my dad's shows were gay.

Therefore, the shoulder-length peroxide permed hair and very warm reception worried me not a jot. Of far more concern was the restrictive size of the flat and the need to walk outside to use the cockroach-riddled shower room. Still, it was cheap, convenient and blessed with a noisy air conditioner.

Instead of carrying out inquiries about my destination before travelling 3000 miles, I now started to discover the facts and history of the Northern Territory retrospectively. First its very existence was constantly under threat from cyclones as it had been partially destroyed in 1897 and 1937, as well as demolished by the Japanese air force in February 1942 by 242 planes. Typically, the Japanese chose a poorly defended mini city with little threat so as to demonstrate their strength. 57 vessels were sunk, 250 people killed according to the authorities (although popular reports suggest up to 1000) and bombing continued sporadically for another 12 months.

It was not surprising that the three-armed forces were represented in Darwin but typically of Darwin, the main naval force was situated 10 miles inland in Berrimah down the Stuart highway and the army close to the sea in Larrakeyah Barracks. The forces have now been expanded and relocated more sensibly. A new presence from the United States has recently arrived triggered by Darwin's proximity to the Chinese influence and the size of Darwin Harbour, one of the largest in the Pacific area – five times bigger than the famous Sydney Harbour.

I slowly discovered the details of the awful destruction by Cyclone Tracey two years earlier. The death and destruction obviously saddened me, but this was not the atmosphere generated by the returning residents and newcomers, of which there were many. I discovered a camaraderie difficult to find even in 1977 – many of us, subsequently, moved around the world but that post-Tracey influx were risk takers prepared to take a break in the Territory to fix it. We still remain friends.

Of course, my first visit was in a sense, accidental, but I soon got the bug. Despite the destruction, lawyers were still needed – it is amazing how many case files with poor chances of success disappeared, 'destroyed' in the cyclone. The newcomers were needed because by the 1980s, over 50% of the 1974 population failed to return.

For the first three months there was little to do except use the local pool, play soggy tennis and work. The work was huge fun – from administrative law to my brief entry into crime! It was a very Territory sort of crime – killing freshwater crocodiles by my client. He had been caught by the Rangers with a substantial harvest. He had fallen foul of relatively new legislation protecting crocodiles, both salt and freshwater species. Until 1970, the croc had been almost shot into extinction in the Territory – a reduction of 95%. The saltwater crocodile was the older variety, with ancestors evolving some 20 million years ago. It was rapid in the water, could swim in the oceans over large distances, exceed 20 foot-long and possessed the strongest bite of any other animal. Its only enemy was mankind, a threat diminished by conservation legislation. This is demonstrated by the increasing numbers; from 3000 in 1971 to currently 100,000. For many Territoreans, the protection has gone too far.

However, the freshwater crocodile was less of a threat, and it was this variety my client had culled under his own initiative. The freshie (also known as Johnstone's Crocodile) grows to about half the size and length and width of the Salty. Unfortunately for the freshie, its bigger cousin is not limited to saltwater and generally breeds upriver in freshwater – there is only one winner. Unfortunately, my client had form and I was appearing in front of the Chief Magistrate known for his strong environmental views. My best was not good enough and the client was handed the maximum sentence of 2 years in jail. As he went down, he was shouting some fairly terminal threats to both the magistrate and me!

Chapter 16
The Monsoon Lifts

For a few weeks in April, humidity built up after the rain stopped but before the 'Dry Season' started. Then, at the beginning of May, the humidity and temperature dropped to daytime temperatures of 30 degrees with the locals starting to wear sweaters and bringing out the duvets as at night-time temperatures dropped to 18 degrees centigrade.

The stingers and cyclones disappeared, opening up the ocean for careful use, and the boats and dinghies came out of hiding, dotting the sea around the Sailing Club. The inland highways opened up, allowing exploration into the bush or 'down the track' as the locals described it. Now the strict monetary limits placed on my expenditure prevented the purchase of a motor car or boat, but it did not stop me freeloading on my very generous friends.

To begin with, I stayed local and was recruited to act as crew on my friend's dinghy, who, unfortunately, turned out to be rather expert having sailed at the Summer Olympics in the Bay of Kiel (off Germany) in 1972. She was the loveliest person in the world unless she was 'Captain'. This was my first sail as 'crew', so I was sworn at and told to hang out as I was only there for ballast. Well, I did what I was told and overturned the boat, not helped by the fact that the tide was out, and the mast got stuck in the mud. A few days later, I had been forgiven and invited to try out her windsurfer – another first for this novice.

I was not entirely useless but by mid-afternoon, I had sailed about 300ft from the beach and could not encourage the windsurfing board to return. I was sitting on the board thinking about a recent story passing around the sailing club, concerning a well-known windsurfer who had recently swept over a 15ft salty, and I was getting very nervous. To my relief, my reluctant mentor came out to rescue me. She tried to get me started with no success and I was towed ignominiously to shore, where it was discovered, I had inserted the daggerboard the wrong way around making it impossible to sail upwind.

I concluded that perhaps the sea was not my strong point, so I decided to latch on to the first weekend bush trip arranged by one of my friends. This happened to be a relatively short trip to Jim Jim Falls in a Toyota Hilux which was a squeeze for three. Jim Jim Falls tumbled over the Arnhemland Escarpment and was at its best shortly after the monsoons had finished. It meant we would need to travel southeast to Kakadu National Park, renowned for the beauty of its natural wetlands, birdlife encompassing over a third of Australia species and fabulous Aboriginal rock art.

We packed our reliable tent into the Hilux and set off – first stop being Fogg Dam. Fogg Dam was not a natural wetland or indeed, a dam proper. It was the residue of yet another failed Territory Dream. Bizarrely, this time Australia's wild north had caught the imagination of an American entrepreneur (Alan Chase), and a future Australian Prime Minister (Harold Holt) who had met at, of all places, at a Hollywood cocktail party in 1950. The two men had different aims: one to repopulate the Territory after the devastation of war, with the white population reduced to 2500, and the other, an American obsessed with a frontier investment. A vast rice paddy was envisaged, with the Monsoon controlled to provide yearlong water for the rice. Cash was provided by a Hollywood syndicate and Federal investment. The RAAF built the Dam, but Territory Rice Limited had seriously underestimated the finance needed due to the seasonal nature of the rain, the rice providing a food supply for the local birdlife and generally the difficulties of developing such an isolated region. It stopped producing in 1964. Although no money was made, it helped develop the local infrastructure, increased population growth and led to permanent wetlands for the local wildlife. It was only three years later that the newly elected Prime Minister, Harold Holt, died mysteriously; described as a drowning accident off the coast of Victoria in 1967. Conspiracy theories still abound.

We reached Fogg Dam as dawn broke to the chorus of the most extraordinary birds, from Herons to Sea Eagles and flocks of the noisiest birds in the world but so typically Australian – Galahs, a grey and pink noise machine living to 40 years old (in captivity up to 80).

Continuing over the Alligator Rivers we headed into Kakadu, which was showing at its wettest, greenest, and most divinely exotic. The prehistoric Tableland rose above the wetlands in the distance and reminded me of all those Lost World adventure stories I read as a kid - particularly King Solomon's Mines. All life poured out of the rich landscape – 1700 plant species, 117 reptile species,

10,000 insect species, 50 freshwater species, 60 mammal species and 280 bird species. With such abundant wildlife it is a shame early explorers introduced a reptile that was not present – there were never any 'alligators' in the Northern Territory, merely the crocs, which were plentiful. It took in four separate river systems, all overflowing their banks in the 'Monsoon Season', and the park area was similar in size to the Scottish Highlands. We were not stopping on this trip at the wonderful Aboriginal rock art sites in the park, who had lived here continuously for at least 20,000 years. This was only intended to be a scouting trip. However, for an 'intrepid explorer', the Territory continued to place the rest of Australia, like the lovely but dull suburbs of Sydney Harbour, in perspective. I was thrilled to be here.

The route along the Arnhem and Kakadu highways was easy going but it all changed when we took the Jim Jim Falls 4x4 track – in a two wheel drive vehicle. The track was severely corrugated and drift sand meant constant changes of direction and digging the Ute out. The Ute did have a snorkel, but we really didn't think we could cross Jim Jim creek and indeed we could not. We had to turn back and settle for Jim Jim Falls – these were all waterfalls pouring over the edge of a plateau. We parked up in the picnic site, intending to camp overnight – in 1975, no one worried too much about where you camped. However, on arrival, I was astonished to find half of Darwin's legal profession indulging in a bush weekend. It reduced the impact of our intrepid adventure but boded well for a good evening. We waded over pebbles and boulders for about three-quarters of a mile and reached a crystal-clear plunge pool with the water rushing over the 350ft cliff. The evening was fun, alcoholic and we then wandered over to our tent, which we had pitched a little way from my friends by the creek. After a short while, we heard rustling and swishing by the edge of the creek. We were sure that they were Freshies, so I spent most of the night wandering about flashing my torch. Next morning, our fellow campers suggested that if we liked strobe lighting that much, we should have stayed in Darwin and enjoyed the only disco. This was typical of several future trips, and I never relaxed, sleeping in the bush.

Chapter 17
A Swift Turnaround –
The Fiat 128

My deal with my companion meant that by June we had to return to the UK – as an Australian, she did not enjoy Australia and particularly, Darwin; as an Englishman, I much preferred Australia and in particular, Darwin. This did not bode well but a deal was a deal. In an attempt to save cash, and the profit-making scheme was indeed highly remunerative, I focused on my job for the first time and the variety was such fun.

One client was an old, injured miner who insisted on giving me a gold watch and an opal ring made from an opal he had dug out! I had a thriving liquor license practice for the major supermarkets. I enjoyed an administrative law practice acting for several of the interstate appointees of the Northern Territory government (for example, the head of the electricity commission) who always fell out with the Toy Town government.

I acted as counsel for both the North Australian and Central Australian legal aid service, providing advice for Aboriginals – particularly the many who were injured in vehicle accidents. They were often single-vehicle accidents caused, sadly, by a drunk driver. My last case got me down to the High Court of Australia (the Australian equivalent of the House of Lords) on the meaning of employment under the Workers Compensation Ordinance, Conair V Fredrickson. The court was shortly to move to Canberra but fortunately, the court was sitting in Sydney, so a good time was had by all (the junior barrister being my predecessor and now mate).

My heart was not in the move back to the UK; I had enjoyed the eccentric legal problems, the money, and the people too much. Upon our UK return, my companion decided that a provincial life was for us – Canterbury. In 1979, you could not get much more provincial! I lasted about 12 months but, in that time, I spent the money I had saved in Darwin on a 17th century beamed cottage and a car at last; a small car with a long name: the *Fiat 128 3p Berlinetta Sports Coupe 1977.*

It was a pretty hatchback with a 1300 engine: typically Italian, needing constant revving. It was a sheep in wolves clothing but had lots of black stripes with Fiat 128 plastered down the side, a completely unnecessary rear spoiler and coloured striped seats with a body coloured in sharp metallic blue. It was everything a 27-year-old could want. It is now a rare car with only 900 odd remaining out of the 60,000 original cars built – it probably says something about the build quality and the sheet metal 'rusting voraciously'. I drove the little car very hard, evidenced by the fact that when I sold it, I was informed by the dealer that the engine was only running on three cylinders!

After a year, my companion and I parted ways, each obtaining something out of the separation – she obtained UK citizenship and I obtained a permanent Australian Residents Permit. Therefore, by 1980, I was preparing to return to Australia with a new companion, who was not an Australiaphobe. I decided on this occasion to take the obvious route in my legal career and fly to Sydney, via Hong Kong, to find a position at one of the major law firms.

I remember clearly the date of arrival in Hong Kong, not because of the fabulous Asian buffet we attended, but because it was the 8th of December 1980, and I was shocked to hear about the murder of John Lennon at the tender age of 40.

Three days later, we were sunbathing on Bondi Beach. Unfortunately, we fell asleep with jet lag and the next day, we had red scorch marks in the most unusual places.

Chapter 18
Sydney and the
Valiant Charger

I had passed through it once and around it twice but never stayed for any length of time in Sydney but now intended to settle permanently. Therefore, after a few days sightseeing, we looked for a modest apartment in Manly. It was the only suburb I had visited, and I had liked what I saw: a suburb with a beach, harbour and a 30-minute ferry ride to Sydney City (or 15-minutes by hydrofoil). What more could I wish for?

The flat I found was modest and it had to be because once again, I was skint and starting my life over – one small living/kitchen room and one bedroom. It did not have any heating – too cold and you opened the oven door. However, it did have a very small balcony overlooking Sydney Harbour and the Italian Coffee Shop was still available, Coles Supermarket had flagons of Australian sherry to make Aussie Pims and casks of Aussie wine. It was a cheap place to live. I registered and obtained the dole for the only time in my life and invested the remainder of my funds in the transport – the ten-year-old *Valiant Charger.*

It was a silver grey two-door coupe with American origins, copying the Dodge Charger (the General Lee in The Dukes of Hazzard). It had black vinyl upholstery and some decent black wheels. It was an early XL VH series with the Chrysler Hemi-6 engine boasting a 4.0 litre engine and generating 160bhp. As it only possessed a three-speed manual, it always seemed a little underpowered, but it looked good for such a small investment.

Whilst waiting for a decent job to appear, we decided to retrace some of my past explorations and head up the east coast to Noosa Heads. We were in no rush to explore Sydney because we thought we will be living locally for a fair while. Of course, I was again short of funds so the usual purchase of the two-man tent took place, although, I hoped to stay at a motel in Noosa. Prior to setting off, I drove on a trial run up to the Blue Mountains. We went to Coles and bought his and hers yellow/red short satin shorts and airtex t-shirts – the height of fashion.

The Blue Mountains are a part of the Great Dividing Range with a peak height of 3540ft. Named 'blue' because of a hazy blue mist which settles over them, perhaps generated by the vast forests of eucalyptus trees. It was an easy 60-mile trip from Sydney to the main township, Katoomba. However, the primary destination was to visit the Norman Lindsay gallery and museum of Faulconbridge which had only opened five years earlier. He was a bit of a hero of mine as an artistic and religious rebel, with a vast output of painting, drawings, sculptures, and books over a period of 90 years, and died as late as 1969. I particularly enjoyed his continued dispute with the arcane Australian church authorities over his work rejecting Christianity and adopting a celebration of nature and the human form. The film, *Sirens*, starring Hugh Grant as a repressed vicar and Tara Fitzgerald as his seduced wife, depicts Lindsay's early battles with the church in 1904. Many of these paintings represented glorious nudes in apparent bacchanalian revelry. They are humorous and full of love and admiration for the human body.

Norman Lindsay was fortunate to live for almost 60 years at his lovely colonial-style house in Springwood and it was this house, he had gradually developed and embellished (concrete statues, works of art, decorated furniture) to make the house an essence of the artist – a lucky man indeed. The visit was well worth it, and we came away with some lovely prints which are still hanging in my house today, including a portrait of Don Quixote and his little squire Sancho Panza.

We returned to Sydney the following day and prepared for the drive north for a couple of weeks. The Charger was faultless, and we followed the Pacific Highway to Noosa, again staying in a motel off Hastings Street on Noosa beach. We explored the local area including Sunshine Beach on the other side of the Peninsula and along the Noosa River towards Tewantin and onwards to Lake Cooroibah and Cootharaba. We fell in love with the hinterland around Malaney with its luscious sub-tropical rainforest and arty community. On one of my later trips to the area, I indulged in one of my least environmentally friendly purchases – 4 stone sculptures which must have weighed half a ton. After the purchase, I discovered that they were not carved in Australia but Zimbabwe in Central Africa. So, bizarrely, they had been transported to the backwoods of Queensland – thousands of miles away. I then transported them thousands of miles back to England.

Chapter 19
A Return to Darwin –
A Special Charger

On our return to Sydney, a position awaited me at one of the better Sydney firms and so holidays were over, and I settled into a pleasant commute to work aboard the Manly Ferry – seated on the deck in the hazy winter sunshine reading a newspaper. I had only been working for 12 weeks and a problem arose with my partner's visa, which only lasted for six months. She was told an extension would be more likely if she applied from an 'outback' location otherwise, she would have to leave the country to apply. Apparently, Darwin seemed to fall into an 'outback' or 'out of Australia' location; so far as the Department of immigration was concerned.

Coincidentally, Darwin came to my rescue again as the law firm which was the competitor to my previous firm was looking for a senior litigator. As I had regularly played tennis with the senior partner, there could be no better qualification. Therefore, the vacancy was filled by me! Therefore, with mixed feelings, I gave notice, moved out of the flat and sold the car – back to square one again. So, including my articles, I had worked for five firms in four years – not a curriculum vitae which would normally appeal to a future employer!

On arrival, we contacted my network of friends and discovered an ex-pom who wanted to lease out his three-bedroom tropical style home in perhaps one of the oldest suburbs; a house with nine foot stilts, louvered windows, a tin roof, and overhead fans. There was always second-hand furniture in Darwin to be had, with 48 nationalities coming and going. We bought some lovely old cane furniture. I repaired the cane and Frances remade the cushions in tropical green. My guitar perched on its stand with movie posters on the walls; we were very comfortable. We celebrated our arrival with a party based upon a fearful champagne cocktail made with the potent Australian Brandy and sparkling wine. One of our invitees was found in the bushes the next morning and taken off to the hospital for a stomach pump – he was a beer man and has reverted to the same.

Of course, the main purchase had yet to be made – another car. I went off to the dealers along the Stuart Highway to find a cheap Japanese runabout. We knew we did not have the money to buy a reliable Toyota Land Cruiser 4 x 4, the vehicle of choice in Darwin, so this purchase was intended as a short-term buy to move around Darwin where public transport was unknown.

True to my intention, I visited the local Daihatsu dealer, but I was side tracked by the part exchange vehicles; in particular a stunning orange Charger of the same vintage as the silver one. However, it was clearly a different beast altogether. This was not a motor vehicle – it was a statement of intent. Black Racing Stripes over the rear wheel arches, a black 'HEMI Six Pack' sticker on both rear wings and a black vertical stripe with 4/RT inscribed. The interior was black vinyl, and I spotted a four-speed manual gearbox. The salesman, large and enclosed in tight shorts and a floral shirt, quickly spotted a 'mark'. However, he did not need to persuade me because I realised it was the king of muscle cars – the *Valiant Charger E49*. It was similar to finding the bottle of Grange Hermitage. As part of the rulebook for the Bathurst 1000 (a 1000-kilometre road race around the Mount Panorama Circuit in Bathurst NSW), the manufacturer had to build over 100 road-ready vehicles to ensure that the race car did not differ in any significant detail from a road car. In this case 149 cars were built and called the E49. A legend was born.

Unlike most powerful cars of the day, it was a 6-cylinder rather than 8-cylinder vehicle with three large Weber carburettors and producing 302 BHP. I discovered; it was said to be the fastest 6-cylinder road car in the world until the 1975 Porsche Turbo 911. It appeared to be in lovely condition, but I was warned that it was a petrol guzzler – hardly surprising with so much power. The car was blessed with a double side pointing exhaust. Further, as it was in essence a race car, the engine carbonised very easily which frequently resulted in some very black faces as the car sped off.

I admit that in 1981 (40 years ago), 'protecting the environment' was not a phrase in common parlance. However, the biggest attraction was that this glorious excess summarised Australia, where everything was noisier and more colourful – even the birds. I paid about the same amount as a new Daihatsu – a few thousand dollars. A similar vehicle was recently auctioned with an estimate of AUS $400,000! After the deal was done, I had only travelled 2 miles and the car stuttered to a standstill – the petrol tank was empty; a common fault of stingy car dealers all over the world.

Fortunately, I had arrived in Darwin with my partner because, for a young man, unattached talent in the Territory was not so thick on the ground – it was a male-dominated society. We had become regular invitees to the Darwin barbecue circuit and began to realise that gentle courtship between the sexes did not seem to be part of the Territory mating ritual. Women stood at one end of the patio discussing Pavlovas and the men at the other end, discussing sport, cars, and fishing – I am not sure I fitted into either discussion group. For the motoring reasons that I have already mentioned, our exit was always dramatic and memorable. However, I was keeping the engine cleaner by regularly driving down the Stuart Highway to a disused air strip to indulge in private drag racing.

It was a vehicle that, in the suburbs, attracted the attention of the police force but generally we had disappeared by the time they had estimated my speed. I had, by this stage, discovered I owned a very special car (perhaps the greatest car I was to ever own) all by accident. Remember, this car was constructed in 1972 and yet, it could hit 60 mph in 5.6 seconds, although acceleration started to level out at 80-90 mph it still had a top speed of 130 mph and the quarter mile in 14.2 seconds. It was awesome and did my image no harm in a city dominated by dull four-wheel drive vehicles. This really was a genuine Australian 'General Lee'. I have a wonderful photograph of the car, perched on the edge of Fannie Bay beach with my lovely companion unknowingly performing the Daisy Duke role – a beautiful dark brunette.

One evening, 'the beast' almost got me into trouble whilst parked. We had taken some clients out to a Chinese meal in Smith Street. I had parked my ostentatious vehicle at the junction with Knuckey Street. When we returned to the vehicle, it was surrounded by police cars and cops. We decided, in our inebriated state, to walk around the block. On our return, they were still hanging around, but impatience got the better of us. Whilst backing up, I felt a mild bang at the rear and a knock on the window. I was requested by a large officer to view the damage. Actually, there was no damage to the beast, but I had knocked out the headlight on the police car. I was asked to take the Breathalyzer, and I knew the result already, but the officer took the results over to a very smooth (for Darwin) detective dressed in yellow trousers and a floral shirt. He called me over and told me to piss off and that I was a very lucky SOB as he had more important fish to fry. I guessed that it was a drug bust and, perhaps initially, they thought my car looked like a drug dealer's vehicle! They allowed me to drive home, and I cautiously edged out to turn right when a group of revellers waved wildly at me and, fortunately, I realised they were warning us not to drive down a one-way street the wrong way. It was a very lucky night.

Chapter 20
The Croc from the
Other Side

It is hardly surprising that some of the most interesting cases I handled in Darwin involved its strange and wondrous wildlife; of course, the biggest and most dangerous was the salty croc. My first case back in the saddle, at my new firm, was an instruction from the other side of the croc fence by Professor Harry Messel; an academic scientist, conservationist and a very bombastic Canadian. He had moved from Canada and became head of the School of Physics at Sydney University in 1952 and set up the International Science School.

When I met him, he was not young but hugely energetic and obsessed with the saltwater crocodiles because, until 1971, it looked as though they would become extinct in Australia. Its continued survival depended on banning hunting (the 1971 legislation) and understanding its habitat. He obtained federal funding to develop habitat evidence, crocodile numbers in particular, and developed maps of tidal waterways in northern Australia – the first time a detailed survey had been carried out. He then promoted various expeditions to carry out the huge task with the reluctant agreement of the Territorean Government.

To some extent, there was a Brexit type divide in the Territory; those who were for the crocs' conservation and others who thought they were dangerous critters who would be better off as handbags. I was somewhere in the middle and prepared to 'live and let live' providing they stayed away from me. The Territory Government was definitely not a fan of the professor, although that may have had more to do with the Professor's deep-held belief, he was being forced to deal with intellectual minnows (probably accurate). He had been granted a scientific licence to shoot magpie geese and catch barramundi out of season for scientific purposes (both species were protected). On the particular survey, the expedition was to keep a tally of the crocodiles, estimates of size and eating habits, not the easiest exercise. To attract the crocodiles, the group shot and fished the protected species and threw the carcasses to the subjects, attracting them to shore. One of the expedition team was a Northern Territory Ranger and, without protesting on the trip, later complained that the members of the expedition were eating some of the flesh from the geese and the gorgeous eating fish, the king of fish, the barramundi. It is perhaps understandable that the group considered that this perfect fish for eating, which had a mild buttery flavour and solid texture similar to halibut, was wasted on the crocodile.

When the ranger returned to Darwin, he snitched on Professor Messel and legal proceedings were brought by the Northern Territory government stating that he had breached his scientific licence. This was extraordinarily petty, and the professor was not going to have some Lilliput government tarnish his reputation. Unfortunately, he initially made the mistake of picking the wrong barrister for the defence. After all, this was only a minor breach of the conservation legislation with a monetary penalty in a legal backwater. He chose perhaps the best-known Sydney Senior Council (QC) to represent him before the Northern Territory Chief Magistrate – this was overkill.

The magistrate rewarded the perceived arrogance with a conviction on all four offences and maximum fines. However, what really annoyed the professor were the gratuitous comments made by the magistrate, to the effect that respected academic should know better. The professor was not a stupid man and had realised that he had made a tactical mistake using an interstate barrister of such notoriety. Therefore, he instructed me to prepare an appeal to the Northern Territory Supreme Court and to recommend a local barrister to represent him. He arrived with boxes of books discussing the meaning and philosophy of science.

We decided that the appeal to the Supreme Court should take the form of an application to quash the magistrate's decision because the Northern Territory Legislation was badly drafted on the three counts including the fact that Melville Island was not a protected area within the Territory Parks and Wildlife Conservation Act. Judge Gallop agreed on appeal with our submissions in the Supreme Court, but Professor Messel did not finally succeed without a variety of visits to the Federal Court and High Court and vast legal bills.

However, his surveys of tidal river systems of the Northern Territory are still relied upon by current conservationists. The crocodiles' success has resulted in the occasional risk of a four-metre croc landing on you lap in a boat as you quietly fish (being able to jump two metres) or chase you around the billabong at 20mph. However, there are far fewer handbags.

Chapter 21
Seasonal Variations

As I sit here in tier 4 lockdown over the 2020 Christmas, I have noticed a distinct irony concerning my life in Darwin and the present circumstances. Darwin, and the Northern Territory in general, is probably the safest place to live in this Covid-19 stricken world - isolated and secure. It is this very geographical isolation and the extreme weather that, for much of the year, Darwin felt like living through a gentle lockdown (perhaps Tier 2). Then we complained – now we would be grateful.

Everything happens in the 'dry season' from May to September. All the visitors arrived from interstate and the sea, and the surrounding bush opened up to those who have been previously patiently locked down by humidity, monsoons, and cyclones. Indeed, the Dry was very similar to the UK summer in 2020; everyone goes slightly nuts.

My second arrival in Darwin was halfway through the 'Dry' but settling into house, job and vehicle meant little time for the usual Dry events, other than a now famous regatta - 'The Darwin Beer Can Regatta'. It was a charity event first held in 1974 with boats made of beer cans sailing at Mindil Beach. After the cyclone it was also a handy way of tidying up the beer cans from thirsty construction workers.

It was officially called Henley-on-Mindil as a tongue-in-cheek reference to Henley-on-Thames and the other regatta held in the dry centre in Alice Springs since 1962 - Henley-on-Todd. The river Todd contained no regular water on which to sail or row - the nearest navigable water being 1000 miles away. Teams ran their vessels along the dry riverbed of the river Todd, which only floods in the monsoon season. Indeed, on the only occasion the riverbed was full of water during the race, the regatta had to be cancelled!

All of this is very typical of the Territory and its inhabitants; namely taking the piss out of any event remotely pretentious and making the most of the extreme geography and climate.

As the build up to the monsoon started (the 'suicide season', 'going troppo' or 'mango madness') we decided to try and buy a house as my dear old Grandad had died and left me £500 cash - not much but with a very large mortgage we found a house in the Nightcliff suburb opposite the high school and one playing field away from the beach. The main attraction was the 500 yds walk to possibly the most glorious public pool in Australia – the Nightcliff pool. It was a 50m pool set on its own with direct views over the Timor Sea enjoying the most glorious dawn and sunset. After we moved into Ryland Road, we got into the habit of arriving at 6 a.m., watching the sunrise and doing our 20 lengths. The only break in the routine might be a heavy dose of lightning as one of the storms rolled in during the monsoon.

The house was typically tropical but small and in poor condition. It had two small bedrooms upstairs and a modest living area with a bathroom set on stilts; a partly built ground floor with an extra bedroom with an outdoor staircase. The extra attraction was a lovely tropical garden with two large mango trees, pawpaws, hibiscus of all colours, pink, red and white bougainvillea, and a large 30 ft above ground pool. It was a very basic water tank, but it did the job.

With the enthusiasm of youth, I set about renovating, painting, creating a terrace under the house and planting the garden. I swiftly discovered the worst car in the world for shifting building material was an Australian race car. I then made the worst possible car decision – I decided to part exchange the Charger for a bright yellow *Mitsubishi* eight-seater people carrier. It was horrible to drive, not even a four-wheel drive but it did carry volumes with a huge sunroof – typically sprouting huge trees out of the top following visits to the garden centre. However, the main mistake was selling the Charger, a mistake I repeated on many occasions; namely selling good cars.

Back to work, I received a phone call from a high-profile insurance law firm in Sydney requesting me to act on a marine case - the loss of a yacht in the Timor Sea. The marine insurers argued that the insured and owner had failed to disclose important facts on placing the insurance; although they really believed that the owner had sunk the yacht but did not have sufficient evidence to prove it.

The legal team from Sydney arrived - partner, the senior and junior counsel. Most southern firms considered Darwin lawyers to be idiots and needing excessive support. Also, it was an excuse for a trip into the northern wilds, sometimes the furthest they would get from Sydney. At our first meeting the partner approached me in a somewhat embarrassed way and asked whether it was possible for his QC to find some female company for the trip. I handed him the back page of the NT News.

However, Darwin was a hospitable place, and it was incumbent upon locals to offer hospitality to interstate visitors, so I invited them to my newly painted terrace for a barbeque. We invited some locals, and everyone was having a good time when the police arrived - very unusual in Darwin. They probably wanted a midnight beer and, following a tinny and a mild admonishment, they headed off. This was then followed by an invasion of fruit bats in the mango trees and aggravated by the intrusion of several aboriginals, also pinching the mangoes. No one really cared and our interstate guests must have thought it was typical of Darwin barbeques. However, even we were surprised by our next arrival, namely a not unattractive blonde with half a usual set of clothes - not exactly ripped but very dishevelled.

The QC was very interested but was rebuffed on the basis that our guest had had enough action for that night. So, we gave her a beer and rang for a cab. We never found out what happened, but she seemed happy enough when she departed. I understand the Sydney visitors dined out on the 'barbeque' for some time.

Chapter 22
An Unusual Liquor Licence

Liquor had played an important role in my life since arriving in Darwin as it did for most Territorians, who could boast for several years as having the highest per capita consumption of beer in the world. Personally, there had been various apocryphal stories circulating Darwin describing an energetic young lawyer found floating in a shopping trolley in the Darwin Hotel swimming pool or jumping across an internal fishpond in a Chinese Restaurant but failing to make it to the other side. This was fairly typical in Darwin.

However, I was making a bit of a career out of it. I have already mentioned how I was frequently instructed in alcohol related accidents – Aboriginals and construction workers. Also, I was instructed by the large supermarkets applying for a license but I had never been instructed to oppose a liquor license.

Therefore, it was a surprise to be approached by a priest, formerly linked to the now defunct Oenpelli Mission. Apparently, the women from Gunbalanya (Oenpelli until 1975) were objecting to a take-away liquor licence applied for by the men of Oenpelli; this was an area on the edge of Arnhem Land and, with several other missions, virtually governed the area for 50 years. However, they did encourage the government to proclaim the 37,000 sq. miles of Arnhem Land as an Aboriginal Reserve in 1931, partly motivated by a desire to keep the area alcohol free ('dry'). The most striking geographical feature was the Arnhemland plateau rising from the wetlands.

I filed the objection and heard nothing further for months. Eventually, my instructing priest told me to close my file as the application had been withdrawn – local female pressure, I suspect. Instead of a bill, I suggested that I was provided with several permits to enter the reserve so that I could lead a little exploratory expedition. I gathered a group of friends, and, with an ancient land cruiser and a Range Rover; we planned our weekend in Arnhemland.

The route to the crossing into Arnhem Land was straightforward – along a mainly bitumen surface and across numerous rivers passing through the wetlands including the McKinley, Wildman, West Alligator, South Alligator and finally the East Alligator rivers – the last being the boundary with Arnhem Land.

At Jabiru, we headed north and decided to stop over at the Ubirr rock formation. It is a spectacular collection of ancient rocks rising above the Nadab floodplain and allowing a superb viewing site. However, the star attractions are the ancient rock galleries with origins of some paintings dating back 30,000 years, although most had been overpainted more recently (if the birth of Christ can be considered recent). The Rainbow Serpent Gallery was fantastic, and, for the indigenous tribe, it is for women only. We were lucky because in 1982, the galleries were less well known and casually restricted, so we had considerable access and time, plus no tourist coaches!

We were now close to the East Alligator border at Cahill's Crossing. As we were in the Territory, the crossing was a challenge. The East Alligator had a five-metre tidal difference in the water level. The crossing was a ford and, on some days, the lowest tide height was three metres. The crossing took its name from another Territorean, Paddy Cahill, who came to the rescue of the local habitat when the water buffalo (which were a wild imported species) were destroying it. He did his best to reverse the process in the 1890s by killing up to 1500 buffalo a month – although I suspect he was the first white fella to settle at Oenpelli and establish a dairy farm – another ambitious Territorean failure. He was clearly not popular with everyone because one of his Aboriginal workers poisoned him in 1917. It is a shame that he could not have built a better crossing before he died!

When we arrived, we were somewhat disturbed to find a large sign warning of 'SHARKS AND CROCODILES' and indeed we could see several medium sized salties (10-12ft) on the river's edge. A cattle truck forced its way across. We let the swell disappear and followed – it was hairy but fun for a suburban lad.

As we headed towards Oenpelli on a dirt track, the countryside opened up. The contrast of the verdant wetlands against the prehistoric granite escarpment rising from the edge conjured up the Hobbits' journey to Mordor. Surprisingly, as well as noisy birdlife, we passed some wild horses – the 'Wild North'. We tumbled into a collection of typical Territorean houses constructed of asbestos sheeting with corrugated tin roofs.

They were built next to a billabong with Injalak Hill, a sandstone monolith, rising three miles to the east, and boasting further ancient rock paintings. The entire area was a vast and wonderful art gallery.

We parked our vehicles and went looking for the Rangers as our vehicles had to be searched and given a clean bill of health – clear of imported alcohol. They were also to lead us to our permitted campsite. We pitched our tents and our knowledgeable 'lawyer bushman' dug a hole for a fire pit and lined it with stone (not river stones as we would all end up pierced by shrapnel). We were also schooled on the type of wood to collect; namely only fallen wood and preferably slow burning eucalyptus. We were advised to avoid hollow logs, partly because they were rotten but also due to the fact that they would probably house a mass of wildlife.

A slab of beef went into the pit but would take a few hours. Normally, this wouldn't be a problem as an esky of tinnies would be opened; cola and coffee did not quite create the party feel. Therefore, after a feed, we declared that an early night was a sensible plan.

After a few nights in the bush previously, without alcohol, I had decided on self-help in the form of some prescribed sleeping tablets – unknown to my companions. A good sleep was had but when I woke up the camp was scattered to the wind, and I found my mates cleaning it up. Apparently, to everyone's amazement, I had slept through a water buffalo mini stampede. I could have disabused them of my coolness but decided that this was the beginning of a bush myth (to be embellished) and kept alive.

The next day we took the short walk to the edge of the sandstone plateau (a mere 5.5 million acres) and about a 1000ft rock scramble to the top. The plateau was very thinly populated by indigenous people, preferring the lowlands, and so we all started telling stories of Lost Worlds – aka Sir Arthur Conan Doyle. When the three of us reached the top, our vivid imaginations ran riot conjuring up stories of a 'first footstep by man' only to find our very own bushman sitting on a rock dangling his feet in the cool clear stream and smoking a joint.

The views allowed us to look along the escarpment for miles. As we returned to the camp, we passed through a dense clump of blackboys and gums, and we heard the deep bass notes of a didgeridoo; we thought we must have stumbled upon a Corroboree. After crashing through the spiky bush, we came face-to-face with a young Aboriginal couple enjoying their proximity with a tape recorder playing 'mood' music.

Chapter 23
Work and Play –
The Alfa

Gradually as Darwin was rebuilt, entertainment venues opened up. The Mindil Beach Casino opened as a huge sprawling building close to the beach, attracting plenty of Asian gamblers. It also provided some good shows and we ventured into the den of Barry Humphries in the front row. This was fine when his alter ego, Dame Edna, performed but the change of character to Sir Les Patterson, a very alternative businessman and cultural icon, led to the 'spraying' of the proximate audience (certainly unlikely to happen in the 'Time of Covid').

The open-air theatre had opened again in the Botanical Gardens where we saw Roy Orbison shortly before he returned home to the Travelling Wilburys (including Bob Dylan, George Harrison, Jeff Lynne (ELO) and Tom Petty). The other bush evening recreation during the 'Dry Season' was the subtle display of 'Monster Trucks'; essentially truck bodies stuck on huge wheels – absolutely mad vehicles. With more conventional cinematic entertainment, good Asian restaurants and always the Sailing Club, life was almost too civilised.

After six months or so, the senior partner of Cridlands, where I had been earlier employed four years earlier, approached me and offered me a partnership to move back and to lead a small litigation team which was to include a South Australian, an Englishman and two Sydneysiders (one of whom I met at my Sydney firm). One lawyer ended up as a leading Counsel in Adelaide, another as a leading Darwin Counsel and then Judge, another Counsel for the largest pearl fishing corporation in the world and another as a marine law partner for an English city firm in Hong Kong. It was an odd place to find such a collection of excellent litigation lawyers, but they were all young, motivated by the profit share arrangement and great fun!

As everyone was competent and keen, my management role was limited, which at 30 was probably lucky. However, my one pleasurable management decision was to invite the team to the Sailing Club, on a good week, for Friday lunch. The task in hand was to fill the trestle table with beer cans and wobble home. We worked over the weekend but somehow it seemed pleasantly rebellious leaving the office early on a Friday. Frequently, my new wife would kindly pick us all up in the Mitsubishi and drop us off, one by one.

By this stage, I was less than happy about my sale of the Charger but that was a ship that had sailed. However, I had found for sale a vehicle even less suited to the Territory as a second car – a *1969 Alfa Romeo 1750 GT Veloce* in Alfa red. It did not take long before I realised that the rear floor pan needed welding and a modest restoration took place in the garage at the corner of Ryland Road. My in-house taxi driver eventually refused to drive it with me as a passenger because the accuracy of the gear changes on the slick, sprung five-speed gearbox tended to be somewhat sticky.

Surprisingly, despite being in the middle of nowhere, the law was hugely stimulating – you never knew what case would walk through the door. This was partly because Darwin was the capital city of a mere 50,000 people but commanded an area of 838,000 sq. miles (or six times the size of the UK). It was considerably closer to Indonesia than Sydney. Indeed, the main cruising yacht race in August sailed from Darwin to Ambon, the capital of the Maluku province.

I kept in touch with the Professor, but I left his case behind with my former firm. One never knew who was coming next – one day I was asked to obtain the first Anton Piller Order in the Northern Territory in a bid to prevent dissemination of pornography. Then the next day to injunct a part owner of a supermarket from entering the premises because of threats of violence to the other partner - two fiery Greek refugees who had immigrated during the Greek Civil War in the late 1940s. Most of the very large Greek population came from Kalymnos as sponge divers and as sailors on the pearling luggers.

Even the professional indemnity work was odd; for example, defending a large international accountancy firm when the senior partner was accused of using undue influence in obtaining the legacy of a substantial cattle station from two elderly owners.

One of the most financially nerve-wracking cases involved acting for an alleged injured electrician in the explosion of a substation. The defendant's insurer would not settle the case and from that fact alone, I deduced that they had some damaging evidence. This particular lawyer loved filming – I think he was a frustrated film director. He was a Canadian and, shortly after this case, headed down to Sydney, complaining if he had to put up with another 'suicide season' he would jump from his own office block.

Anyway, I started thinking hard because I had persuaded my firm to fund the litigation. The main loss concerned his inability to earn a living as an electrician – future loss of income. Clutching at straws, I sent him off to a psychiatrist to provide an opinion as to whether this fairly dramatic accident could have created a mental block preventing his ability to undertake similar work in the future. Joy of joy, he provided a positive opinion.

My opposition lawyer, fuming, made an application to prevent us using the report as I was serving it late, only months before trial. However, he also wanted to fly my client around Australia seeing a variety of specialists. Now this was a tactical mistake – judges do not like it when insurers try to have 'have their cake and eat it'. I argued that my client should only have to see one specialist and the specialist should be taken to my client – not the other way around. This would allow two tactical advantages; first, it would result in one expert for each side, and it would probably result in the insurer's expert being a hack medico legal expert at such short notice – the real experts would be busy practising their real profession in their home State. A kindly judge agreed with my submission and the medical appointments were limited to one expert each – 'one-all'. It is still used as a precedent in the Northern Territory after 40 years. The stubborn insurers refused to settle, and the trial proceeded.

In the end the trial, judge believed our client and expert, determining that it was entirely understandable that, when someone is almost obliterated by a major explosion, he may have some concerns in the future. Incidentally, this was despite the fact that the insurers had some very good film of my client working underneath his caravan involving a fair degree of flexibility.

As to the missing yacht, we had stumbled across the most indecisive judge in Australia – he took months/years to come to a decision. He even invited counsel to attend Darwin to hand down the judgement and then changed his mind!

Chapter 24
The Land

A superficial inspection of the Territory would suggest that there is not a lot upon which an entrepreneur can capitalise and indeed, many ambitious schemes have gone awry. However, there is an awful lot of land with a very small population and therefore, it is cheap.

The two primary land-based industries were mining and livestock. The Territory was never as rich in minerals as its Western Australian neighbour, but it had its own Gold Rush in 1870 bringing over many Chinese workers, until Darwin was wiped out in 1897 by cyclone. However, some returned and, when I became an Australian citizen in 1995, it was in front of a Chinese ethnic mayor and his two companions – one Filipino and the other Scandinavian, which was typical of Darwin.

The mining industry still included gold, but manganese and uranium became important by the 1980s. However, my senior partner was a particular favourite with the cattlemen and so some disputes came to me. The Northern Territory 'station' (cattle ranch) was much closer to the US Wild West than Herefordshire but wilder and larger. Originally, the land had been a free grant of land to brave pastoralists. Today, a list of the largest cattle stations are only included if they cover in excess of 1500 square miles. The largest in the Territory was Alexandria Station established in 1877 with about 10,000 square miles or two-thirds the size of Wales. There were five founding fathers forming the North Australian Pastoral Company which over the next 150 years acquired many smaller stations over different habitats to sustain it through drought – many more in Queensland than the Territory but the Alexandria remained the first and the biggest.

The 1970s had not been a happy time for the cattle industry. Success as always depended on price, volume, and the market. Weather and disease brought the industry to its knees. The soils were poor and the climate rarely balanced. Frequently, the problem was not drought but too much rain in the Victoria River

Dams and Barkley Tableland, washing away the soil's nutrients. The soil was better quality further South but the land more likely to suffer from drought.

As to disease, the cattle were riddled with Brucellosis and Tuberculosis and the BTEC campaign was introduced, requiring stations to fence their properties at huge expense, which many stations were unable to support. A beef depression and high interest rates were the 'final straws' for marginal stations. Even in 1900, Banjo Paterson summed it up, 'With the Cattle':

> *The drought is down on field and flock,*
> *The riverbed is dry;*
> *And we must shift the starving stock*
> *Before the cattle die.*
> *We muster up with weary hearts*
> *At breaking of the day,*
> *And turn our heads to foreign parts,*
> *To take the stock away.*
> *And it's hunt 'em up and dog 'em,*
> *And it's get the whip and flog 'em,*
> *For its weary work is droving when they're dying every day;*
> *By stock-routes bare and eaten,*
> *On dusty roads and beaten,*
> *With half a chance to save their lives we take the stock away.*

However, in times of gloom and doom, there is always one optimist, and he was our senior partner's VIP client. Peter Sherwin was his name, known as the Cattle King. A rags to riches story – he was a drover and son of a drover. He became Australia's largest private landowner with 17 cattle stations and running about 300,000 cattle.

He started buying more properties in the late 1950s in the Victoria River District and Barkley Tablelands. The marginal stations presented acquisition opportunities at relatively low prices in the 1970s and 1980s. Not satisfied with rejuvenating the industry, he operated a large cattle transport company. He formed a tough negotiating team with George Cridland, our senior partner; five years ago, he was still in the law business whereas I had retired despite being many years younger. They make them tough and smart in the Territory.

My most dramatic involvement in the industry was brief but vital. One morning, George strode into my office and asked me to be in court that afternoon. Apparently, a winding up petition was to be heard concerning Elsey station not paying its debts. Elsey was relatively small but an icon of the Territory, being romanticised by a short-term resident Jeannie Gunn in the book 'We of the Never Never'. She had accompanied her husband, Aeneas Gunn, a minor explorer, to the Territory where he managed the station for just 18 months and in 1901, died of dysentery. His wife returned to Victoria and wrote a book to titillate suburbanites with misty-eyed tales of the outback. Although famous, Elsey had never been lucky; with its original founder, Abraham Wallace, killing himself 18 months after his stock had arrived 'being tired of this world and the world is tired of me'. Early mortality and financial impoverishment continued to curse the station.

Crack-brained schemes like the Eastern and African Cold Storage Company led to its abandonment in 1908 and, although subsequently reinvented, Elsey was never successful and was even the location for a murder in 1968. A manhunt finally ran to earth Harry Boy who had axed the kitchen hand, Marjorie.

My instructions were that the substantial sum of money owed by Elsey could be paid that afternoon when a telegraphic transfer arrived from Hong Kong. Fortunately, Mr Justice Muirhead was sitting (who I will discuss later) and he was a relatively long-term judicial appointment in the Territory, a delightful and caring man and upholder of The Territorean Myth. A judge for over ten years in Darwin and finally the Administrator (equivalent of the Governor General) of the Territory, I would, I hoped, get a sympathetic hearing from this legend.

My target was to adjourn the hearing for a few days to allow the money to arrive. Unfortunately, my instructions were incomplete, and I had not been informed that this was the third time that the petition had been presented, with excuses made by the Station and requests for adjournment which had been granted. Unsurprisingly, the Court was not inclined to grant me any adjournment beyond close of court business at 4:30 p.m.

Regular phone calls and reports to the Court were made all afternoon and 4:30 p.m. approached with no firm news from Hong Kong. Even Judge Muirhead was irritated and gave Elsey one last chance by keeping the court open until 5 p.m. 15 minutes before the deadline, I could confirm the debt had been paid! In 2000, the Station finally reverted to the original occupiers of the land if not the station – the Mangalayi people.

Chapter 25
Dingoes and Other Wildlife

We were in Darwin through the trial of Lindy Chamberlain and, although not involved in the case, we knew many of the lawyers who were involved. For those whose memory is short, Ms Chamberlain was accused of murdering her young baby whilst camping by Ayer's Rock in Central Australia. The Chamberlains had alleged that the baby had been killed by dingoes. No motive could be discovered, and the body was never found.

However, the Chamberlains' behaviour had been slightly odd after the death; they always failed to dramatize their grief, perhaps because of their beliefs and connection with the Seventh Day Adventist Church. In the usual media stampede for headlines, accusations were made of baby sacrifices and other such rubbish. However, despite no eyewitness evidence and doubtful forensic evidence, the jury found the Chamberlains unanimously guilty, and Judge Muirhead had no option but to hand down a life sentence.

I think the overall view of the legal profession was 'guilty'. I was rather doubtful about the conviction, believing the Jury had read too many headlines. Unless the Chamberlains were completely mad, what on earth would cause apparently decent human beings to take a young baby on a camping expedition and kill it in the middle of nowhere; instinct suggested it was twaddle.

My reservations were proven correct when the evidential tale took a turn in 1986 when this odd case ended in an odder fashion. In a search for a climber who had fallen off Ayer's Rock – he was found, sadly dead, but in an area renowned for dingoes and the baby's lost matinee jacket was found. Finally, all convictions were quashed. None of this could be blamed on Jim Muirhead; his summing up was as fair as possible.

My only involvement was frequently walking past the camera outside the Supreme Court Building hoping to get a picture on the telly for Mum and Dad; a ruse which failed miserably.

We had been in Darwin for about 18 months and decided to spend a few weeks during the Monsoon in the summer in Tasmania – three weeks travelling around a lovely island in a gentle summer (the opposite of Darwin). Many travellers make the mistake of underestimating the variations in climate in such a vast country, summed up simply stay away from the North between November to April and vice versa for any area South of Brisbane.

Whilst away having a lovely motoring trip, always my preferred choice, we left the house in charge of friends – a decision we would regret. My recollection of Tasmania is of an extraordinary variation of landscape in a relatively small area. The wild south-west displayed rough mountain ranges and rainforest; the North around Launceston suited the country lane lover or anglophile; the East coast was a lovely gentle coastline reminding me of the Mediterranean without the crowds; the central Highland with 3000 lakes and finally Hobart and surrounding bays and creeks.

Halfway through the trip, we telephoned our first caretaker and queried if there were any problems. He responded that it was fine although we no longer had a swimming pool! Apparently, a strong swimmer, he had kicked off from one end and he surfed out onto the road with 10,000 gallons of water! The entire above ground pool disintegrated.

When we returned, the house was in a state of chaos – obviously the night before our second occupier had organised a hell of a party without our permission. In addition, they had failed to note the day we returned correctly so the clean-up had not taken place. Not the end of the world – after a clean-up and a prompt insurance claim – but not ideal.

Our next encounter with Territory wildlife came on a weekend trip to Katherine – a township of 6000 inhabitants known as a cattle centre, an intersection for 2 highways and the closest town to a lovely gorge; formerly known as Katherine Gorge but recently renamed the Nitmiluk National Park. It included the sandstone gorge carved by the Katherine River and the Edith Falls.

We arrived at our campsite, pitched our tent, and went out on an afternoon cruise up to the fifth gorge. Not a great bush sleeper, I was up at dawn the next day for a morning jog, staying away from any water as the river was home to plenty of freshwater crocs and the odd saltwater one left by monsoon floods.

Following a track, the jog away from the camp provided no surprises. However, shortly after I turned back, I heard running footsteps and breathing behind me. Now this was not Hyde Park, and it was extremely unlikely that this would be a fellow athlete. Too insecure to turn around, I went faster and slower, but the steps followed at whatever pace I adopted. As, with some relief, I entered the campsite I slowed down and an emu almost the same height drew alongside me and looked me straight in the eye. Subsequently, talking to the manager, this was a party trick, noting my running partner could run at 30mph. The Encyclopaedia Britannica lists it as one of the six most dangerous birds in the world, together with the Ostrich and Cassowary, although I am sure I saw my new acquaintance winking at me!

Chapter 26
Mums and Dads

The Dry Season always attracted incoming relatives who were not always prepared for the Territory wildlife which, to be fair, was some of the most lethal in the world. Some of the least attractive and most dangerous were imported, including feral pigs. Pig hunting was a regular occupation for those who enjoyed guns.

The biggest and the most destructive to the natural environment were imported water buffalo. Huge 1000kg herbivores, with occasional bad moods, were introduced in the nineteenth century for hauling and tough tucker. They created channels in the grassland which led to saltwater contaminating the glorious freshwater wetlands. They were kept under control by buffalo hunters like Paddy Cahill but are now culled by aerial shooting. In the 1980s, they were being culled for the BTEC campaign but there were still enough around in 1983 to be a nuisance. Eventually, reduced to 250, they have now increased to 150,000 – particularly present in Arnhem Land where they are virtually unmanaged.

Square set with enormous horns by which they can gore a man terminally, there are many deaths recorded. Between 1825 and 1843, 80 water buffalo were brought to the Cobourg Peninsula and Melville Island, where attempts were made to settle in Port Essington. As one of the few large game targets for hunting, it became embedded in the Australian Mythology with hunters like Joe Cooper being dubbed 'The White Maharajah of Bathurst Island'. He first visited Melville in 1895, greeted by the Islanders, he kidnapped four of the Tiwi people, treated them well and learnt the language. When returning, he sent his captives forward as the greeting party and settled with his indigenous wife whilst culling 1000 water buffalo a year for 10 years; he also become known as the 'King of Melville' island. The buffalo hunter even received a few poetic lines from Banjo Paterson who joined several expeditions:

Out of the big lagoons,
Where the Regia lilies float,
And the Nankin heron croons
With a deep ill-omened note,
In the ooze and the mud of the swamps below
Lazily wallows the buffalo,
Buried to nose and throat.
From the hunter's gun he hides
In the jungles dark and damp,
Where the slinking dingo glides
And the flying foxes camp

The Cobourg Peninsula is still virtually uninhabited but there are a few ruins at Port Essington. It was originally an attempt to establish a marine link with Asia. Convicts were sent, a mission established but the usual problems in the Northern lands caused eventual abandonment after 20 years – disease, climate, and cyclones. However, for present day sailors it was an attractive destination, despite predatory crocodiles of some size and water buffalo. Close to the peninsular is also Melville Island which again supported feral buffalo, providing meat and income from trophy hunting.

Good friends of ours decided to sail to these destinations one 'dry' with their parents – not so foolhardy because all were fit and fine sailors. Unfortunately, on a brief landing on Melville Island the father caught a buffalo unawares and was charged and gored. Suffering severe injuries, the expedition was able to contact the authorities and a helicopter rescue was made off the beach. Swiftly airlifted to Darwin hospital, he was lucky enough to recover and still going strong at 93 years old. Sailing the yacht back, the party looked over the railing and sighted a black saltwater croc swimming alongside and swore it was almost as long as the 32ft hull. Few crocs have been found of that size but who knows! It is certainly a reminder of the dangers that lurk below and above.

As I was neither a sailor nor a bushman, the entertainment I provided to my parents, when they surprisingly visited after four years, was more modest. It must have been a dramatic change for an aged matinee idol/operetta tenor and his wife, who had spent much of her life in the leafy suburbs of Walton-on-Thames. I was rather proud of them, particularly Dad, when he assured me that he could well understand the attraction of the overhead fans, tropical climate, and lush vegetation as it reminded him of all the Somerset Maughan short stories – validation is always acceptable. The reality of tropical living must have become apparent when, in the morning, they found about 20 dead cockroaches on the bedside table which had 'enjoyed' a few surplus sleeping tablets.

However, we all decided that they should have one trip outside Darwin before they left, involving an overnight stay at a hotel in Kakadu. The first part of the expedition was intended to be an airboat trip from Mary River Bridge and Boat Ramp on the highway to Kakadu. However, an earlier incident rather overshadowed the planned events. Shortly before the destination, Dad and I decided that we should relieve ourselves but just as we were finishing, we caught sight of a good-sized water buffalo running towards the bright yellow van with some rapidity. We stumbled into the vehicle just as the beast charged from the side. Fortunately, I had left the ignition on, and it just missed us as we sped off, as fast as a not very fast van could go. In my rear-view mirror, the buffalo was standing astride the highway looking rather pissed off and dim.

Again, Mum and Dad took this confrontation in their stride and awaited the next torture. We had already 'enjoyed' the airboat cruise, so we shipped the parents off on their own. When they returned, Mum's Walton-on-Thames perm had been swept into an astonishing confection.

Onwards and upwards to the next stop – the newly built Jabiru airfield to take a short flight over the edge of the escarpment, avoiding the need for rough four-wheel drive exploration. For the first few minutes, all was fine, as the weather was clear and gorgeous views were head of the waterfalls. However, suddenly the little plane started to disconcertingly fall and rise, confirmed by the pilot to be caused by thermal columns of rising air. Unfortunately, one little member of the expedition had been fed too much chocolate and brought it up all over Dad.

The previous year a baby addition had been made to our family and my lovely mother-in-law was determined to fly out and visit us. A grande dame raised in an army family in India, we anticipated she would fit into the Darwin way of life with ease. My father-in-law would not fly, being a good deal older, and having vowed after serving in Burma in the Second World War never to set foot in another plane. So, this was Peggy's first overseas trip for many years. It was a cheap flight with a stopover in Denpasar, which we were all a little concerned about. She arrived safely, however, with a tale to tell. Peggy could have stepped out of a Miss Marple film; all lavender and soft white/grey curly hair and apparently naïve (I was never so sure). At the London airport, she had been asked by the travel courier if she could take a parcel with her and drop it off at an address in Denpasar. She could never say no, so in due course delivered her parcel undetected by customs and without any idea as to its contents! The address was located in the back streets of Denpasar and when her task was done, she asked where she was to stay overnight and apparently no one had the faintest idea but suggested she could stay upstairs. Her bedroom had no glass in the windows but had a mosquito net. Settling down for the night, she swiftly realised from the noises that she was sleeping in a brothel. However, her innocence got her through, and a taxi was organised for her the next morning.

It was wonderfully amusing to hear her describe, on the phone, to her concerned husband, Colonel Gordon, that the accommodation and service had been first class. Bless her as she also took control of the household enabling us to take a vacation in North Queensland which I had never reached in my travels. A fellow partner at my law firm had a beach house between Cairns and Port Douglas. It was more of a cabin, made of wood with a corrugated iron roof – rough and ready but the location was worth a million dollars, and it was free! We kept our eyes open for crocs and had a much-deserved rest.

Chapter 27
Cyclones and the
Top End

As part of the 'build up' and 'wet' (November to April) a further descriptive term could be used – the 'Cyclone Season'. Darwin lay smack bang in the middle of most of the cyclonic depressions with several passing close by each year. In 1897, Darwin, then called Palmerston, was obliterated and in 1937 there was a repeat performance. It is not surprising that to the locals life always seemed temporary. The puritanical inhabitants of the Southern Australian States had long since decided the sinful population of Darwin (probably true) had brought the Wrath of God upon themselves.

However, by 1974, there had been a generational gap of 34 years without a major hit. Buildings had been erected without consideration of cyclone codes and generally the locals ignored the risk.

The ABC (the Australian broadcaster) had announced that Cyclone Tracey was passing, although it broadcast that it posed no risk. The cyclone suddenly changed direction, reaching 135mph at least (because some instruments failed) and it tore through the poorly built tropical homes. The population was particularly vulnerable as defences were down celebrating Christmas. Most of the population had to be evacuated and 71 people died. It also destroyed 31 aircraft and various vessels. The public statement at the time summed up the devastation:

'Darwin had, for the time being, ceased to exist as a city.'

Many inhabitants never returned but many others arrived to rebuild the city and I suppose, without intentionally doing so, I was one of these newcomers. Some stayed to become the Territory hierarchy whilst others re-joined their lives elsewhere frequently complaining that the pioneering spirit that had existed for

10 years, following the cyclone, disappeared and Darwin reverted to its status as a small tropical city. By 1980 the city was largely rebuilt with a new layout, building style and code and a new population. I suspect the population turnover is still high which gives the place its originality. It is very difficult to be parochial if you are likely to move the following year.

We had been lucky with cyclones whilst in the Territory and, although there had been several near misses, we had become rather blasé. Therefore, it never occurred to me to worry when it became necessary to travel to Perth to prepare for a trial concerning my client who was a paraplegic claiming damages for an employment injury on the oil rigs offshore. We settled the case just before Trial, but I stayed over with friends to enjoy a couple of dinner parties. It came as a surprise on the evening of April 12th to receive a newsflash on the ABC that a cyclone had hit Darwin, although there was limited information. I was now panicking and could not get through to the family, feeling very guilty that I was not looking after them. As it turned out, it was a weak cyclone with very little building damage and no casualties. When I finally contacted the gang, I found that, equipped with bread, hard-boiled eggs and cokes, they raced down the road to the cyclone shelter in Ryland Road High School, sharing their tucker with other evacuees.

When they returned to the house, they found it full of leaves, branches, and green ants, which en masse can be dangerous from a venomous bite. They were not so common in the North – we must have collected the whole population together with the usual extras, including cockroaches. By the time I returned, the clear up had been largely completed but I definitely felt there was more discussion about moving on from Darwin, although I still loved the place and the work.

Whilst in Perth, I had been approached by the opposition firm and asked whether I would join them. It was a branch of Freehills in Sydney to whom my original reference eight years prior had been directed – what comes around goes around. Schooling was an issue for the children - Darwin was not noted for the quality of its schools.

The alternative was a return to the UK (Frances and I were both missing family) or, just possibly, Sydney. However, if I were to move, I realised that if I wanted a traditional career in a larger city, it had to be soon as I was 33. I had pushed my luck successfully, but I knew I had to stick with Darwin for my career or move. Many of my friends stayed and have been very successful – QCs, judges, chief justices, administrator etc. As I approach 70, I do wonder whether I would have enjoyed that life more. Perhaps we all have a moment in our life which changes us for good – this was the moment for me, for better or worse.

We decided on a compromise – to try out Perth; my second go. Again, it was made easy by my arrangement with Freehills whereby we gave each other six months to decide if the move would suit us both – if it did, I would become a partner, if not I could leave.

Chapter 28
The Trip to Perth
in the Yellow
Bumblebee

As usual, I managed to sell up everything in record time and by the end of 1985, we were ready to say a sad farewell to our friends, most of whom have stayed friends. Of course, we could have flown down in a few hours but when I could drive, I always drove – my love affair with the motor car still intact.

I had sold the Alfa and so it was the yellow bumble-bee van (as named by our daughter) which would take us the 2500 miles from Darwin to Perth. I now calculated I have driven at least 15,000 miles in Australia.

As we set off the 'Build Up' was starting – hot and humid. It was not only us that suffered. We found out that on long journeys, one could either enjoy air conditioning or move forward – we could not do both! So, we had to ventilate with hot air and dust; made worse by the fact that some of the roads on the journey were unmade, and our transport was not of the four-wheel drive variety.

The first leg of the journey was the short trip to Katherine and then West. The first stop was Kununarra, a township, which had expanded with the construction of the Ord River Dam in the 1960s creating Lake Argyle and the irrigation for over 30 farms. We next reached the Kimberley region, now in Western Australia. It is a remote area, about three times the size of England, full of stunning rock formations with gorges and plateau style mountains with a maximum height of about 3000ft. If the reader would like a pictorial view of the Kimberley's watch 'The Circuit' – a dramatic recreation of the travelling court which travels around the Kimberley Region. The coast, virtually unpopulated, was subject to a Japanese scouting party in 1944, without the Australian armed forces even knowing of their arrival. Presumably, they decided the terrain was too difficult to invade.

As usual, I did not have enough time to investigate the area properly and, with temperatures close to 40 degrees centigrade, there was some imperative to make haste. We had a look at Lake Argyle and Emma Gorge as they were close to the highway. However, our first stopover was at Halls Creek which was, without doubt, the least attractive township I had come across in Australia and the least attractive motel. The current photos of the motel show no resemblance to our truly awful room (improvement over 40 years) which the four of us inhabited with a defunct air conditioner and yours truly sleeping in the bath. On the other hand, the restaurant was truly unexpected. With temperatures outside close to 40 degrees centigrade, the restaurant was dark, chilly and with a Swiss or Austrian wooded appearance. We ate delicious Wiener schnitzel with a bottle of dry Australian Riesling. The food made the room tolerable for one night. Next stop was about a seven-hour drive to Broome via Fitzroy Crossing.

Broome, on the northern coast, was the centre of the Pearl Fishing Industry and the Paspaley fleet. We had met some of the family in Darwin; one of our good friends is currently their in-house lawyer. Old timers in Darwin described it as the town Darwin used to be in the good old days and frequently threatened to move there.

The two towns enjoyed similar experiences in the Second World War with Broome also bombed by the Japanese 4 times – they really liked easy targets. In March 1942, 86, mainly civilian refugees, were killed and 22 boats destroyed. It also had the same climate and seasons – including the vulnerability to cyclones. On arrival the town had a certain tropical charm and a lovely 15-mile beach, Cable Beach.

After a good night's sleep, we planned the rest of the 1800-mile trip with two further stopovers and a fried van. The family was looking forward to seeing its new house. Previously, I had spent a weekend in Perth and casually bought a pretty 1930s bungalow in South Perth on the other side of the Swan River. I wanted to commute by a ferry with a walk at either end.

The remainder of the journey was uneventful, although later, I received a speeding ticket for driving 62mph (clocked by a police helicopter) in the middle of nowhere, on empty roads, in a van with a dodgy engine. The Australians adore bad boys from the past, Ned Kelly or the first convicts, but in reality, they are suburban and love rules and signs; even in the middle of the bush. Unlike in the UK, the Aussies obey the rules – perhaps it is to satisfy themselves that they are now law-abiding. It reminds me of the tale of a friend who, on disembarking, was asked whether he had a criminal record whereupon he replied that he did not know it was still required.

Now, it may seem a little impetuous to buy a house and furnish it when I only had a six month commitment from Freehills. It was even more impetuous to give a home to a large fluffy cat, build an extension and buy a new car all in the first three months. My dad always said that I would be exhausted when I reached 60 years old because I went at life like a bull in a china shop – he was quite correct.

I wanted a car which complemented the white lattice work on the house with trailing roses and bougainvillea and an elegant 13-year-old *Mercedes W108 fuel injected 280SE* caught my attention. This one was one of my good buys with about 145bhp and a top speed of 116mph. It was the vertical twin headlight American version, but right-hand drive, in cream with tan vinyl upholstery; very elegant and relatively cheap. In the short time we owned it, there was not a single problem.

Life was pleasant and we labelled the city as 'Perfect Pink Perth' (PPP) but in the time we added an extra P – parochial. Perth was a long way from any other major conurbation and, in the 1980s, the average Western Australian was very defensive about his or her pretty city. We found it very difficult to keep our tongues in our head. Even though Darwin was so much smaller than Perth everyone knew it was not perfect – for goodness' sake, it had been wiped out 10 years before and with a 60% changeover of population. A newcomer was welcomed and embraced – 48 ethnic races were present plus the indigenous population. It was an odd place, whereas Perth wanted to be considered another mini-Sydney or Melbourne but better.

We enjoyed the beaches, coffee in Freemantle, picnics in South Perth Park (fighting off the seagulls with Frisbees) but it was very tame. The work was fine but not challenging. At the end of the six months having bought our house, extended it, bought a car, grown attached to a cat and found schools, we had to decide whether we wanted to stay. The UK had the attraction of family and, with London, possibly more exciting work but would I be welcomed back at 34 years old? There would be no 'This Is Your Life' return as the prodigal son. It was going to be a tough job remaking my career after the fun and friends of Darwin. However, my ego was big enough to want to test myself in the biggest legal market, other than New York, and we did miss family. We had the advantage of a nest egg earnt in Darwin to help augment my income. It was toss up: move to Sydney or a return to the UK. Finally, we decided on the UK.

Chapter 29
A Return Home –
A Jaguar XJC

A return home: well in reality Darwin was more home than the UK and I suppose I never got over the move despite the demanding Territorean climate. I had acclimatised to the heat and, even with our return in English summer, I suffered from the relative cold and caught every possible bug, almost losing all my teeth in the first six months.

However, as usual, well in advance of our arrival, I had already decided on another unsuitable car for a family – a Jaguar XJC. These were the two door versions of the XJ saloon which were pillarless creating a lovely silhouette but needing the everflex to cover the poor welding. It was built in small numbers between 1977–79 – the British Leyland period! I should have been on notice – rust, rust, and more rust. In the first week, I located a 19784.2 black XJC with a black everflex roof and red leather upholstery – it 'looked' good. As Dad was still a Jaguar man, I took it off to his house in Shepperton-on-Thames to show it off. He was impressed and offered to pay for a fill up of its two separate petrol tanks in the petrol station dead opposite. Taking advantage, I popped across the road, but it seemed to take ages to fill the car and then I smelt petrol! Gasoline was flooding from under the Jag – one of the tanks had rusted through. Much to my (and Dad's) embarrassment, the garage had to close, and the fire brigade called to clean it up. Another success story for the British Motor Corporation.

With one usable tank, we drove to Kent to stay with my brother-in-law. I went shopping with two women and two kids, only to be stopped by a police car on suspicion of being in a 'get away' vehicle – they clearly had some odd gangsters in Crowborough.

I now made the biggest mistake of my life as I agreed to settle near my in-laws in the seaside town of Whitstable. It was tatty in the way of all English seaside towns but quaint because of the fishing harbour but a two-hour commute to London by a tedious train journey. Of course, as soon as the family became settled with school and grandparents, I was stuck, and the next six years were the toughest in my life.

Mind you, my usual employment luck came to my rescue. 1986 was in the late Thatcher years and the economy was booming with a desperate shortage of experienced lawyers, particularly transactional specialists. As every lawyer converted to commercial law, there was also a need for litigation lawyers and although my career had been unconventional, I had undertaken pretty well every sort of litigation.

I was not attracted to the major city commercial firms after the ones I had worked for in Australia because the litigation department was always the poor relative of the commercial and corporate department. Indeed, client contacts came through the commercial departments who were jealous of their client relationship – there is nothing worse than being instructed by some other smartarse lawyer! It was also a harder path to partnership as the easy money was always through corporate deals where fees could be charged proportionally on the size of the deal rather than hours worked. Remember, this was 1986 and there were a lot of deals around, including privatisation. I was just about to accept an offer from one of the big boys when, thankfully, I was asked to interview at an old insurance firm (established 1840) Barlow Lyde and Gilbert. It was medium sized but, as a specialist insurance firm, one of the largest in the world. I was to find that the insurance legal profession was a global village and easy to make (or break) a reputation.

For a 'court lawyer', it had numerous advantages; one of which was that as a litigating firm, the litigators ran it. Also, insurance contracts generated their own regular litigation naturally. It could be defence litigation, acting for the insured (e.g., ship or owners, professionals, property owners, personal injury claims and others) and also coverage disputes between the insurer and the insured. As insurance contracts are a special contract, said to be based on utmost good faith, there is a one-sided obligation upon the insured to disclose any information which might have influenced the underwriting judgement of the insurer. Although the insurer had a similar obligation; it was usually the insured who would have the factual knowledge of the risk. In the case of Carter V Boehm, as long ago was 1776, Lord Mansfield, probably our greatest civil law judge, established the key principle of Utmost Good Faith. In this age of Scottish Nationalism, we hear a good deal about the deeds of outlaws like Rob Roy, exaggerated by Sir Walter Scott or Mary Queen of Scots and her sad execution at the hand of the evil Elizabeth (ignoring the fact that she fled Scotland to avoid death by her own countrymen and played a hand in nearly every attempt at dethroning Elizabeth). Yet nothing is said of those talented Scots who, subsequent to the establishment of the Union, brilliantly advanced the cause of the Enlightenment.

William Murray (Lord Mansfield to be) epitomised this ambition. A son of a Jacobite family, he was educated at Westminster; to which he trekked the 360 miles on a pony at the age of 13! Despite being known by many as having Jacobite leanings, he was accepted for his brilliance as judge, peer, politician, and advisor to the King. His judgements and legal interests included slavery, freedom of the press, crime, and punishment, women, and marriage and, of course, commerce and insurance. A man to be proud of by any nation but I suspect most SNP voters have never heard of him or if the name rings a bell, he is dismissed because he was a successful Scot in London, not Scotland. He is certainly my hero!

Carter V Boehm contained two characteristics of insurance which would attract a 'relatively' young lawyer' – the facts were unusual and international.

Mr Carter was the Governor of Fort Marlborough, built in Sumatra by the East Indian Company, and he insured the Fort against being taken by a foreign enemy. Of course, the telephone, telegraph and the internet did not aid the collection of information by the insurer. Mr Carter failed to inform the insurer of the particular weaknesses of the location. He knew that the fort could resist a native attack but not from a European Power and he knew it was likely that the French would attack. Presumably, this is why he insured it for its commercial owners (note, not the English Government). Lord Mansfield decided that this was almost fraud, but not quite, so he invented the new principle of Utmost Good Faith.

The importance of the case established a body of insurance law in London long before any other country in the world. The law was frequently copied internationally, and London expertise was recognised globally, encouraging international cases to be litigated in London. The law developed conjunctively with market practice in the London insurance market. Therefore, the use of market experts in court cases are still used today in pure insurance and reinsurance law.

So, the early development of insurance law went hand in hand with the early commercial development of insurance based on Great Britain's trading and maritime activity. Frequently seen as the home of insurance, the innovative Edward Lloyd opened a coffee shop on Tower St (and then Lombard St) in 1686 where he actively encouraged merchants and ship owners to meet. The business included passing over parts of the risk of a voyage to insurers, thus sharing a risk. It was very similar to gambling, but it was Lord Mansfield who provided these adventurers with some contractual protection and some commercial credibility.

These insurers adopted the name of the coffee shop – 'Lloyds'. As an organisation, it was a fairly loose affair, moving its location on several occasions until the *Lloyds Act in 1871* which allowed the Market to write larger risks. Unlike corporations, it was dependent upon individuals (usually wealthy) to put up capital and guarantees to allow 'the underwriter' to insure. The Names, as they were called, then received a share of the profit.

This was easy money when things were going well but the very, very big losses could bankrupt a name without the protection of incorporation. The San Francisco earthquake in 1906 and Hurricane Betsy almost destroyed the Market. However, nothing had prepared it for the 1980s and 1990s when a combination of catastrophes and long-term losses (primarily under Reinsurance contracts) changed Lloyds forever.

Lloyds was an oddity due to historical development, but most insurers adopted incorporation, although they had to abide by strict capital requirements.

Chapter 30
New Firm, New Department,
New Law

I have mentioned the term 'reinsurance' and some of this chapter discusses what this means because it is to play a part in the next 14 years of my legal life. However, if I have strayed too far from the motor car, please pass to the next chapter.

The department for which I was being interviewed was relatively new and, more unusually, practising a new type of law – reinsurance. The reader, I suspect, knows about as much about reinsurance as I did, although coincidentally, I had been involved in one reinsurance claim for the Territory Insurance Office before I left Darwin.

This ignorance is hardly surprising because for over 100 years, reinsurers had been keen to steer clear of lawyers. They had drafted their own contracts and if there was a dispute (heaven forbid), it would be decided by a commercial arbitration judged by market experts (not lawyers) and to be governed by good faith, dispensing with strict rules of evidence.

For this to work, this 'club' had to be small enough for the members to know each and every loss to be of a manageable size. The key to the reinsurance business for Lloyds and the large European Reinsurers, such as Munich Re, Swiss Re and many others, was honour and trust.

So, what is reinsurance? Your insurer may underwrite many thousands of risks (e.g., personal injury, professional indemnity, property, and other types) but may not have financial capacity or capital to pay all the claims. Therefore, it has to buy extra capacity by passing on part of the risk to Reinsurers. In turn, Reinsurers might pass on some of their risk to the next in the chain, Retrocessionaires, and so forth.

A variety of different types of reinsurance contracts would achieve different account protection but, at a basic level, they were either described as Treaty or

Facultative Reinsurance. The former covered the insurers entire portfolio (or part of it) whereas facultative usually covered one large risk, particularly large property, or construction risks (for example dams, power stations, mines, and many others).

Treaty Reinsurance was primarily divided into proportional and excess of loss; the former led to a percentage amount being passed onto reinsurers whilst the latter was used for claims above certain levels. Therefore, the latter was better suited to catastrophic losses.

The facultative contract was also used by large corporations to avoid tax and allow them to avoid direct insurers by opening up the reinsurance market. They achieved this by establishing their own insurance company subsidiary in an offshore location, most of which I visited over the years (such as Guernsey, Isle of Man, Bermuda, Cayman Islands, and others). These new 'insurers' were called 'captives' and they were generally run by captive managers, frequently linked to the larger insurance brokers. The captive then reinsured into the reinsurance market.

The insurance broker was the other important player in the market. Each link in the insurance/reinsurance chain required selling to multiple markets (Companies or Lloyds). Generally, it was the brokers who were the creators of these deals, the primary duty was owed to the insured.. Each level of contract might have multiple participants with the one with the largest share (usually) acting as the lead underwriter. He or she, together with the broker (depending on the working of the leader clause) would determine minor disputes/claims. However, on most major issues, a market meeting was required to obtain agreement from all participants. At that meeting with a Scandinavian, German, Englander, French, Italian, Swiss, US and other participants, the lawyer hoped to reach a unified decision. It was far harder than prosecuting or defending the actual case, with many millions of pounds at stake. We are told not to pigeonhole national characteristics but, in my experience, most national representatives offered few surprises; the French refused to agree on principle, the Germans and Swiss wanting everything in writing and the British and Americans had the most in common – including a similar legal system based on common law, precedent, and an oral tradition.

So, if the Reinsurance Market did its own thing, why was there a sudden need for a specialist Reinsurance Department? This was largely due to three factors. First, the market had expanded to include many more and much smaller companies – the relationships which formerly existed were less secure with the newbies and they were too small to pay large claims without investigation. Second it was the time of the binding authority where major insurers in London or even Scandinavia would authorise underwriters elsewhere to underwrite business without proper controls and also remunerate them on the basis of premium income rather than profit. Indeed, by the time all the claims had been generated, two or three years down the line, the mobile underwriter had probably moved on to cause damage elsewhere.

Finally, the claims in the 1980s were so large not even the old boys, like Lloyds, could sweep them under the carpet with notable Names becoming bankrupt. It ended up with litigation between Lloyds and some of the Names alleging fraud which the Court determined was unproven but did state that there had been staggering incompetence and sloppy practices had existed.

The bottom line was that the Lloyds Names, Corporate Reinsurers, Binding Authority Participants, Brokers, and Regulators all started to use lawyers and Barlow Lyde and Gilbert was the first in line. When lawyers were presented with contracts and arbitration clauses drafted by non-lawyers, they found there was plenty of room for dispute; some contracts were so awful as to be almost indecipherable. Many of the losses may have been expected, such as the European storms, Piper Alpha, but the long-term losses from the asbestos liability claims from the US were not.

I had an odd interview for the position on offer because it was in two parts. The head of the new department was absent for the first interview. Instead, I had a delightful chat with a slightly embarrassed newly made-up professional indemnity partner. Again, coincidentally, we had a case in common as he acted for the London insurers who insured the global accountants I acted for Darwin, due to the alleged misdeeds of its senior partner. It is indeed a small world, and it gave me confidence that this was not an insular firm.

The second interview was again easy going with charming interrogators, including the main man, Colin Croly. The most judgemental comment was made by Colin when he suggested my career had been peripatetic, an accusation with which I could hardly argue; he might have said ramshackle. My main impression was a thorough lack of pomposity and decent guys. Two of the interviewers were South African and I later found there was a large contingent in the firm. Some discussion was made about a review for partnership in the following April, but I treated it like Perth – I did not want firm commitments either way. I have always considered a job interviewee is judged by his own opinion of himself – best not to be over enthusiastic about promotion. If you demonstrate talent the rest will follow – relaxed and confident is the name of the game. This was not an attempt at manipulating; I never really cared that much about status, although I did expect to be properly paid for a good job.

Chapter 31
The First Year Back

I will not beat around the bush – the first year back was hell. First, I could never get used to the cold and spent the next six months ill. I remember, in December 1986, sitting in the Tower of London gardens at lunchtime muffled in heavy coat, scarf and gloves feeling (and obviously looking) thoroughly miserable. I was accosted by Colin's wife who was passing, and she remarked that I looked so down in the dumps that perhaps I should go back to Australia.

I was keen to show my worth and was working with about four or five different partners in a variety of departments. This was intended to allow them to assess me for partnership, but it all drew income into the Reinsurance Department from elsewhere. I was involved in a Treaty Reinsurance dispute in the Reinsurance department, and I could prove the worth of a mixed legal background because a defamation case arose out of it. As I had advised the ABC in Darwin as their Territory Counsel, I was used to the peculiarities of libel law. The QC I instructed in Darwin to appear in a libel case ruefully informed me that it was the first time he had ventured out of Sydney and its coastline. He had travelled to Europe and the States on many occasions but not in Australia. This was not unusual, as many Australians did their 12-month trekking overseas before they had explored their wonderful and huge island. Mind you, to be fair, I had travelled to a far greater extent in Australia than Europe.

Of course, in addition to health and work, I had to travel an extra four hours a day by train – which I hated. The commute was entirely unreliable – I am a car man. One has no control of the train or the passengers who sit next to you. The carriages were dingy, dirty, cramped and on occasions it was impossible to find a seat on the return journey. In the winter, one left home in the dark and returned home in time for bed. Early in my commuting career, I started chatting to a distinguished elderly gentleman who admitted to 40 years of commuting – he was a Lloyds underwriter. To prove the present incompetence of Rail

Companies, he described the steam trains he first commuted on. They were non-stop, took less than one hour (instead of an hour and twenty minutes) and had a lovely restaurant carriage in which you could order a silver service breakfast – so much progress!

My worst journey was so bizarre as to warrant a Mr Bean production. It was January and I had to be in Amsterdam for an early meeting, so I had decided to stay in London with friends. Halfway through a pleasant evening I decided to check my papers for no particular reason. What did I discover – no passport? I rushed off and returned to Whitstable by 12:30 a.m. but needed to catch the 4:30 a.m. to get back to London. Unusually, the train guard inspected my ticket and to my horror, probably due to tiredness, I had left my wallet behind with my season ticket, bankcard, and sterling. I had my plane ticket, Dutch currency, and a passport. Fortunately, the guard believed me, perhaps on the basis no one could invent such an idiotic story.

At Victoria Station, I changed some currency to sterling to get me to Heathrow. On arrival at the departure desk, I received the good news that Amsterdam Airport had closed for fog. With difficulty, I switched to a plane for Rotterdam which was still open, although the plane arrived an hour and a half later. I then had to get from Rotterdam Airport to Amsterdam by train and by the time I reached the Dutch Lawyer's office, I was three hours late, the meeting almost over.

So, a sandwich and back to the airport but this time, to Amsterdam because Rotterdam had closed. Of course, I had changed my ticket for departure from Amsterdam to Rotterdam and had no reserved seat. Three attempts to board planes ended in failure and Amsterdam Airport appeared to be my bedroom for the night. Finally, I was allowed onto the last flight out arriving too late for my train to Whitstable and so I resumed my stay with the London friends, arriving at a very fashionable one o'clock in the morning. Somehow, I never organised my travel arrangements successfully and however good the hotel, I always ended up with a view of the car park – there must have been other views.

On a trip to Boston, however, a relatively senior partner showed me how it should be done – chauffeur to the airport, first class air travel and a five star hotel. He impressed me as to how he could still complain about the service interminably. The case was a commercial arbitration determining coverage for our client, as US Reinsured, making a claim for asbestos losses from the London market. The case was delicate for Barlows because usually, we would act for the

London Market – now our opposition. I was still learning the ropes concerning Reinsurance, but I was happy preparing any case for court (or in this case commercial arbitration).

My primary lesson, however, was how to use barristers cleverly in the UK, particularly senior barristers (QCs); namely it should be 'horses for courses'. Subsequently, if I used barristers, I would adopt the role of the theatrical agent choosing my star for the right part – nobody is good at everything. Does the role demand a mastery of detail or the law? Does the advocacy require first class cross examination of factual witnesses or professional experts? Did the case need sophisticated submissions on the law? Very few lawyers could manage all these skills with an equal degree of success – particularly cross examination. This was partly due to the fact that our Commercial Bar focused on large and complex cases, usually headed by a QC who would undertake the advocacy. This was a Catch 22 circumstance in that they may have had very little trial work before taking Silk because, as junior counsel, they would be focusing on the same tasks as their own junior counsel; namely dealing with a document heavy case and researching the law (Catch 22).

Therefore, I often found that if a case required the barrister to break down the testimony of key witnesses, without being too nice, I may use a leading counsel with criminal law experience. The junior counsel and I would prepare the legal submissions.

In this particular arbitration the senior partner had instructed one of the most brilliant barristers at the commercial bar. He has since been appointed to the Judiciary in all our Civil Courts at an extraordinarily early age. However, it was clear to a hypercritical Australian import (me) that, as they say, he was not 'on top of his brief' (probably from overwork). By his closing submission, he had caught up, but it proved to me you didn't always need the most brilliant lawyer in an arbitration which may have not been that newsworthy. However, what do I know because until recently I would have said that the barrister who had most impressed me was a young Australian QC, Marcus Einfeld, who had appeared in the Australian High court on the Conair V Fredrickson case. He had everything one might admire in an advocate – physical presence, a superb fluency, a mastery of detail and an ability to pick up legal issues swiftly. Not only his legal and judicial career impressed but he served as an 'Ambassador for Refugees', a UNICEF 'Ambassador for Children' and was named by the National Trust of

Australia as an 'Australian Living Treasure' – one of only 100 people deemed to have made an outstanding contribution to Australian society.

Then apparently, he must have had a 'brain fade' by perjuring himself and creating false evidence to avoid, would you believe it, a speeding ticket! Not only that, but he was also only 6mph over the limit. He was given a jail sentence of three years (of which he served two years) and most of his honours were removed – pretty tough for a man who had given such honourable service previously.

By April 1987, I was knackered but getting on top of insurance and reinsurance law. I was invited to attend a partner meeting where I assumed I would be told whether I was to be offered a partnership; I had sort of decided I would accept if offered. I attended and sat outside the conference room for hours and I could hear that in the conference room there was a degree of loud debate. It showed how little I cared about becoming a partner (half hoping I could return to Australia) because I just got up and walked out, informing the secretary that I had waited long enough.

I found out later that the debate has been about another proposed partner because the proposer had failed to mention that he intended to marry the particular person. I was later informed that my proposal was passed without debate, and no one noticed I was absent – everyone wanted to go home. Generally speaking, I found over the years that most partnership meetings were equally pointless and Christmas parties dangerous, leading me after a few years, to dispense with my attendance at both. This was my most obvious failing – I was not at all clubbable, politics were not my forte and I could not stand bullshit.

Chapter 32
Acquisitions – The Saab,
Land Rover and MG

My second partnership changed my life in a way my partnership at Cridland and Bauer had not. The latter had always seemed temporary in that eventually, I would pass through. Partnership at Barlows appeared to be permanent because I was heading towards middle age at 35 with a mortgage and family to support. Indeed, I remember on one grey and cold winter's day walking along Whitstable beach despairing over the predictability of my future – a future I had managed to postpone for 34 years. Many would say I had been very lucky noting that I had only lost a year or two in promotion to a city partnership despite having rock and rolled around Australia for 10 years. However, on that particular day I did not feel lucky.

I would only be a salaried partner rather than enjoying a share of the profits (as an equity partner), so I still retained some freedom. However, my pay had increased, and I was allowed a firm car paid for by the firm. I was still feeling constricted by England after the wide-open spaces of the Territory. The semi-detached Victorian house in Whitstable was fine but provided no garden worth mentioning. Somehow or other, we were chatting to a builder who said that a house with five or six acres of land had just come up for sale a mile outside Whitstable. Now readers, do not be under any misunderstanding that Martell Lodge was a manorial estate. It was many things but never smart. However, it did have space and a lovely aspect of Golden Hill in the summer. It had obviously been a chicken farm because of the abundance of wire netting stuck in the grass; it had been a home to horses evident in the truly ugly corrugated iron stables and a hay barn because there still existed a 40ft wooden structure leaning at 20-degree angle. The land was extensive but consisted of untamed paddocks and wild orchard – not a flower in sight.

It also became apparent that the builder had known it was for sale because he was undertaking work on it following the 1987 gales. On our inspection, we found one of the horses trying to enter the rear sitting room. A problem which became apparent after our purchase, when my mother found she had fleas after sitting in it. Even without the damage, this was the strangest house I had ever visited. It was constructed entirely of concrete in the 1930s, making re-wiring almost impossible. We were told that the house had been constructed originally on land owned by some aristocrat or other to provide a home for his slightly mad nephew who was fond of arson. True or not, the entire building was concrete with metal window frames. It had a large ground floor with a substantial flat roof, and apart from one large first floor bedroom shaped like a triangular Greek temple at the front with mock pillars. The only other first floor space was a galleried two storey hallway.

It was odd enough to attract us, gave us the space and I had to give credence to my dad's prediction by adding yet another load to my existing work burden. Mowing five acres, even with a sit on mower, is not much fun. It also provided space for as many cars as I could afford – so I started off with three.

The Jaguar XJC had ceased to exist, always destined for a sad end, it had been taken for a joy ride by a 15-year-old family member who shall be nameless. It ended up in a ditch broken in half. We bought our first Saab 900 which was a white and fuel injected with automatic – primarily for the family. For fun, I had purchased a lovely 1966 MG in British racing green and with wire wheels it felt a lot faster than it performed with a 1798cc engine generating a mere 95 horsepower – 0-60mph in 11 seconds on a good day. However, it had the correct colour, chrome bumpers, the wire wheels and of course a convertible, which meant it looked the part. I have had a few more small sports cars, as we will see, but I always preferred the larger vehicle. For 'farm' work, I bought a very cheap Series 1 short wheelbase Land Rover. On made up roads it was liability – a gearbox which barely had synchro-mesh and it was held together by rust. It was, however, very useful around the rough acreage pulling out wire and rubbish. A good quality example could fetch £25,000 in this present market, although with the best will in the world my purchase would have cost more to restore.

So, a workhorse it remained, and I felt very macho and Australian.

This was the start of acquiring cars rather than just buying for necessary transport. Obviously, I had more cash, but I think it was a substitute for the motoring adventures I had enjoyed previously. The small (very small) holding was highly inappropriate for a commuting City lawyer, but I think it kept my feet on the ground, closer to the wilds of Australia.

We had a few motor accidents through this period but the oddest was during a very cold winter in 1990/91 when, although one mile from Tesco, our lane could become totally snow blocked. Attempting to drive the children to school in the snow, I saw a police car about 100 yards away along our narrow lane. I gently pressed the brake pedal, and I could now see the police driver attempting the same – ever so slowly we drifted into the mildest of front on collisions. On this occasion, I did not get prosecuted!

Chapter 33
Specialisation

My legal career had dramatically changed in two years. As a Darwin lawyer, it was the constant variety which challenged and amused. I was now a partner in a highly specialised department within a specialist firm which was, of course, the way to become an expert. Within these limitations, we were amongst the best in the world and in a real sense creating new reinsurance law.

However, I always seemed to attract marginal work as well perhaps because of my previous history of covering most areas of civil law – nothing really fazed me. Over the next 25 years, my main areas of speciality encompassed reinsurance litigation, work concerning industrial property insurance, insurance coverage work, drafting insurance and reinsurance contracts, subrogation, the defence of claims against insurance brokers and drafting agency agreements, binding authorities, and other agreements for the market.

The work for other departments continued including assisting on a case known as Superhulls. The firm always had a stronger client base in the non-marine Market (property, casualty and professional indemnity) than marine, however, in this case, we were acting for the Marine Market against our usual clients, the non-marine London market, who had reinsured their Marine colleagues by a one off Facultative contract because of the size and value of the so-called 'Superhulls' oil tankers. The middleman was the insurance broker, as was so often the case. The Marine Market had settled the original claim with the tanker owner for US$300 million; from memory this was the largest hull claim in the Lloyds Market.

I have mentioned that quaint market practices would astonish other commercial clients (including their lawyers) in any other transactional enterprise. The insurance policy in this case insured a vast sum of money in the 1970s/1980s and yet it was completed (underwritten) on a Slip Policy. In any other field of enterprise, extensive and legally drafted documentation would have determined the rights of the parties. However, a slip policy was used in reinsurance contracts in London allowing the reinsurance brokers to present a document of two or three pages long with the rights and obligations represented by shorthand market phrases. The slip represents the deal until a full contract document was agreed between the reinsured and the reinsurer; drafted by the insurance broker.

It would be obvious to any onlooker that such an arrangement leaves the deal open to many difficulties of interpretation. What happens if the loss occurs before the wording is agreed? How do you interpret the shorthand? What happens if the parties cannot agree to the wording? What happens if there is a dispute, and one party asserts that the Slip Policy and the wording do not match (as was the case in 'Superhulls')?

In this case, the team from Barlows was slightly odd in its composition as one might have thought it would be handled by either the Marine Department or Reinsurance. However, the Marine Department was small with no reinsurance experience and the Reinsurance Department was only just emerging, so it had fallen to a professional indemnity lawyer to lead the case but a good enough litigator to have pinned down the insurance brokers to very helpful written statements.

However, despite my position in the Reinsurance Department, my role had little to do with Reinsurance. Rather, my task was to prove that the settlement made by our clients was reasonable. This should not have been an issue if the Non-Marine Market (defendants) had admitted that it was a reasonable settlement, or the Reinsurance contract had a well drafted follow the Settlements Clause.

First, the non-Marine Market refused to concede the reasonable nature of the settlement and there was not a well drafted clause in the agreement – which if it had existed would have allowed our client to agree to a settlement with few limitations. Also, they could have obtained agreement from their Reinsurers pre-settlement, but this did not occur.

In the absence of any of these alternatives, the contract of insurance and contract of reinsurance stood independently, and we had to prove the amount of the underlying loss as if there had been no settlement at all.

This appeared to me to be pointless waste of legal costs, but who was I to argue? Particularly when it required a trip to New Orleans where the settlement had been made. My job was to take statements from the lawyers and experts involved. My hosts were welcoming, perhaps partly because I represented an important London Market, and it was their work I was scrutinising. The Senior Partner, however, definitely had his share of old Southern charm and we stayed in contact for years, with family visits to Martell Lodge. I was taken to view the antebellum nineteenth century houses decorated with vast Greek style columns and verandas all built on the back of slave labour in the plantations. However, the glorious oaks, untainted by slave guilt, and covered in parasitic mistletoe, were the real stars.

Perhaps one of the best nights I had on any business trip was club crawling around the French Quarter of New Orleans listening to a variety of blues and jazz, fuelled by an excessive amount of bourbon, and accompanied by most of the firm. Late in the evening, the older members headed home and by 12 a.m. there was just me and the youngest partner. He suggested that we move out of New Orleans into the country, and we entered a building which looked like a barn. Indeed, it was a sort of barn but with a gallery, stage, some fantastic blues and not a white face; certainly not a white face dressed in suit and tie. I persuaded my companion to remove them, and we settled in for the rest of the evening. When a little worse for wear, I did enjoy 'singing along' and although I say it myself, it is in my grandfather's bass-baritone which is quite suited to the blues. After an hour or so, a large group of audience members moved, rather worryingly, towards us. However, delightfully, it was to complement me on my blues singing voice. It was the best compliment I ever received – John Hanson Senior eat your heart out!

These trips away were a pleasant break from the daily grind backwards and forward to London. In this case I stayed at the lovely Royal Sonesta, filled with wonderful American art. However, as usual, I went for my early morning jog and on my return, I had my usual chat with the concierge who inevitably informed me, with relish, that I was lucky to return alive when I informed him of my jogging route.

Exactly the same thing happened when I travelled to South Africa on a case involving the interpretation of Bankers Corporate Policy. The meeting was in Johannesburg, a city noted for its dangers even in 1989 and again, I went for a jog, apparently in life threatening areas. This scenario was repeated every time I travelled but up until now, I returned safe and sound without damage to my personal wellbeing.

One of the best sources of work for international insurance lawyers was the binding authority. Insurance may appear to be a global product but unfortunately, it is regulated separately in each jurisdiction – in the US that often means each State. It is also expensive to set up an insurance business in an overseas location. Therefore, frequently with the creative genius of the insurance broker, an individual underwriter will choose a type of insurance business, provide an office and team. The broker will then identify a local insurer which is authorised to insure the insured business and then reinsure the main part of risk to an international reinsurer.

This was particularly attractive to the Lloyds Syndicates which were not generally equipped to set up overseas offices. However, by taking a large share of the premium income also meant accepting the losses. The primary weakness of this arrangement was that the party most likely to suffer loss (Lloyds) had the least control over the underwriting, and yet underwriters operating the binding authority were generally remunerated by the amount of premium created irrespective of whether it insured good quality risks.

I became involved in one such binding authority and bizarrely the underwriting took place in a beach resort in South Carolina, insured into a Chicago based insurance company and reinsured into Lloyds of London. One might have though some warning bells would have sounded by the type of business, namely US trucking. It required me to spend many weeks and months in Chicago not just for the Trial but for many mini trials in Chicago called depositions. The US deposition is one the most expensive parts of litigation because, unlike the UK, a party is allowed to interrogate any witness under the control of the opposition, under oath, prior to Trial. Some depositions can take weeks, as it did in this case.

I loved Chicago and formed a good relationship with my Chicago lawyers who chose a wonderful hotel for my stays, the Intercontinental Chicago. The main attraction was the architecture and magnificent 1930s swimming pool. It had originally been built in 1928 and I was fascinated by the various decorative styles – it was very much a Freemasons Lodge. I discovered that it had been built by the Shrivers as the home for the Medinah Athletic Club. It incorporated Assyrian and Moorish styles, including a gold dome. When built, it included a miniature golf course (indoors), a shooting range and the fabulous 33yd swimming pool in a magnificent hall (which still existed for me to swim in).

Unfortunately, the Shrivers never got to swim as they had to file for bankruptcy in 1934 following the collapse of the share market.

It finally became a hotel in 1944 and the movie star swimmer, Esther Williams, swam in the pool and Al Capone practised mini golf! As luck would have it, the hotel had just been restored by Intercontinental before my arrival and thank you Tom White, probably the most cultured lawyer I met. An English Literature graduate who studied under Saul Bellow at Chicago University, he knew more about architecture and art than any other person I had met. This is appropriate as the modern architecture in Chicago is magnificent. It also benefits from a delightful art gallery, the Art Institute of Chicago, which has a wonderful collection of impressionist art comparable with any French art gallery other than the Musee d'Orsay. Evenings were spent at Chicago Jazz Clubs or large noisy Italian restaurants. On weekends, we took in the wonderful Chicago architecture like the Tribune Building or jogging down to Lake Michigan where one had to compete with lethal cyclists, roller skaters, skateboards, and scooters. The city, however, was dominated by the overhead rapid transit system, or the 'Chicago L' best known for the 'Blues Brothers' car chase under the supports (destroying 60 police cars) and the noise which is ingrained into every Chicagoan. My friend, Tom White, stayed with us in the Kent Countryside and brought with him a tape of Chicago rail and road noise to play at night – he could not sleep in the quiet.

Chapter 34
Cars, Cars and
More Cars

As our house was improved with extensions on the first floor, new sewers and drainage and a new drive to the second field, a gale finally demolished the old barn which was fortuitous because the insurance claim allowed it to be rebuilt. With a rebuilt barn, I could house up to four cars and with a further two garages, the real obsession with collecting started.

We always had one sensible firm car which was the Saab 900; it was followed by a black Saab Turbo but matching an automatic with an eight valve engine made it one of the most dangerous cars I ever drove. As an automatic you could not hold the car to increase revs to 2500 which triggered the Turbo. Therefore, it displayed horrible turbo lag, with a delay before it moved from a standing start and when the Turbo kicked in it headed off like a scalded cat.

Then came the *Jeep Cherokee* period (green, black, and silver), which was a punchy and petite four wheel drive (by present standards). Great in the snow, it never let us down. The MG had been sold to pay for a trip to Darwin and to Cairns – leaving the kids with my mother-in-law. This time in Cairns, we expanded our horizons with a motoring trip around the Atherton Tablelands and tours up to the Daintree Rainforest and Cape Tribulation, named as such by James Cook when his ship, the Endeavour, ran aground on a reef, now known as Endeavour Reef. He is reported to say that this area 'began all our troubles'. I remember more vividly attempting a pee in an outdoor loo and being surveyed by a huge funnel-web spider – about the only poisonous spider not common in the Northern Territory.

On my return, I boosted up our car numbers by buying a pimento-coloured **Triumph TR6** and a crimson **Jaguar XJCV12** with everflex roof and black upholstery. You will remember, I did not have a good experience with my black XJC and that had been with the less troublesome 4.2 engine; the V12 was already famous for overheating. When you opened the bonnet, you would view the most complex looking engine you would be likely to come across in a road car, but there was no rust. It was a good car and another car I sold far too early and would now be worth about £30,000 to £35,000.

On the other hand, I was glad to get rid of the TR6. It looked good, sounded great with the 2.5 litre engine, 150bhp and 0-60 in 8.2 seconds but I was not used to a manual or lack of power steering. It started off badly and got worse. I bought it at UK Sportscars, then in Littlebourne, now in Wingham. I took delivery of the vehicle, turned right and right again (with some difficulty with large mag wheels) and put my foot down. Unfortunately, there was a sharp right-hand bend which I did not make and went straight into a field. I had to walk back and ask for help to pull it out! However, as the collection was increasing, I rarely drove it and so felt I should give it a run out on a commute to London. Without power steering, automatic or air conditioning, and sitting in the usual queues up to the Blackwall Tunnel, I vowed never to drive it for any distance again – its writing was on the wall.

I was now thoroughly fed up with the train, made worse by a series of bad winters. We were wandering down Tufton St in Westminster when we saw a handwritten postcard in a mansion block window offering to sell a flat at a very low price. This was a period of property slump, which do occur. Everyone assumes property prices will always increase – memories are short. We were just 'looking' but a smiling caretaker jumped out of the doorway and asked if we wanted to view it – obviously on commission. It was a lovely little flat overlooking South Square and St John's Concert Hall. I was now an equity partner and bought it for the grand total of £90,000 on a large mortgage. An investment and a bolt hole for me. I banished the horrors of the train commute and on the occasions when did commute from Kent, I used a car from my eclectic collection. Westminster proper in 1991 was not trendy or expensive for Central London. Other than MPs and the Peabody Estates, anyone with aspirations headed to the Mansion Blocks in Victoria or further on to Chelsea. I was always attracted to a slightly tatty environment, Darwin, Whitstable, Manly and elsewhere. It was full of government office workers but few residents although it was very convenient.

Our village (all inner London suburbs are villages) grew up around Westminster Abbey and historically developed as the political centre and the

City of London as the finance centre – my commute became a drive along the embankment between the two. For centuries, much of Wesminster housed a mix of the very poor and affluent. Social Welfare and slum clearance had reduced extreme hardship but there were still huge wealth gaps between the privately owned and subsidised accommodation. On the other hand, there was little difference in quality between my little flat and the Peabody Estates. As a result, Westminser always seemed very safe and pleasantly mixed. Sadly, this all changed from 2000 onwards when the developers found Westminster and sold the new flats off plan to Chinese and Russian investors.

However, my life was getting easier – it had taken six years from our return.

Chapter 35
Education and Entertainment

When I first undertook my training in 1975, the legal profession was banned from advertising and marketing was required to be subtle – the cosy drink or lunch with a client but not huge social events. However, in the very year I returned from Australia, the profession joined the Thatcher Years and 'subtlety' went out of the window. It is an old-fashioned criticism but I think we sold out the professional relationship and the trust/loyalty that went with it. Advertising parties and every other wheeze was now utilised. Lawyers became commodities, selling themselves to the cost-conscious insurance market.

However, the alcoholic client luncheon was still popular amongst the London Insurance Market – indeed the consumption of alcohol in the market was still acceptable in any form in 1986. I was invited to a luncheon in Barlows own dining room (shortly after I arrived). Our senior partner and an infamous Lloyds' underwriter were present with alcohol flowing. I stayed until mid-afternoon but left to deal with some work for a couple of hours. When I returned at about 6 p.m. the port still flowed, and the waiter was sitting down at the table drinking and debating rugby – no one had noticed. On another occasion, I was invited to a dinner to celebrate the settlement of some contentious litigation with all of the protagonists present, including the primary culprit, the insurance broker. Towards the end of the meal, after considerable overindulgence, I noticed the rogue broker slinking over to the underwriter with a slip of paper (a slip policy) and the underwriter scratching it. He had committed himself to a risk over dinner through the same agent he had been fighting with for several years.

In 1986, no self-respecting firm would overtly advertise but it was gloves off for any other form of marketing falling into two main categories: education and entertainment. On reflection, my department probably overemphasised the 'education'. If you are not careful, you can educate not only your clients but also your competitors, particularly as the department was creating a new body of law. Maybe we were a little naive.

One event was unique to Reinsurance; the Rendezvous in Monte Carlo which was not entertainment or education. Once a year, in September, members of the insurance and reinsurance industries met in a very informal fashion in the coffee bars and restaurants of Monte Carlo. It is an opportunity for representatives to get to know each other personally and reinforce the trust that was the key to a successful reinsurance industry.

By the mid-1990s, the Rendezvous had been active for 34 years and traditionally lawyers and other industry service providers had not been present, or indeed welcome. However, times had changed and Barlows had become an important part of the industry in sorting out its legal problems, being voted the 'Best Reinsurance Service Provider of the Year' amongst other awards. Therefore, we were one of the first legal teams to have the impertinence and know-how to set up our own stall in this glamorous location.

It was a lovely place to be in September and I cannot pretend it was a chore for the first couple of years. A helicopter flight from Nice to Monte Carlo and a three day stay at the glorious Hotel Hermitage Monte Carlo, with its lovely pool and beach club.

Yes, some meetings took place on the beach. Was it worth all the expense? On reflection, it was really a case of being present to avoid competitors filling the vacuum. The novelty wore off for me after a couple of years; I was not good at repeating client events. Our summer event was taking a box at the Goodwood Races for the four days. Again, it was fun for a few years but gradually boredom set in.

I was more enthusiastic about education. If I was honest, it was more to do with academic self-promotion rather than being a frustrated professor. The most demanding project undertaken by the department was to write a loose-leaf book for the first time focusing on Reinsurance Market Practice and its interaction with the law – Reinsurance Practice and the Law. It was written by the whole department and, as well as our personal contributions, Michael Mendelowitz (another partner) and I edited it for several years.

As my years at Barlows progressed, I became less interested in Reinsurance Law and more excited by insurance problems which had a connection with industry – I had a fascination with heavy engineering and the challenges of learning about the technical peculiarities of each process. The types of disputes generated by industrial property insurance largely fell into coverage and subrogation litigation.

Coverage disputes were between the insured, usually a large-scale industrial corporation, and its insurers. Frequently, this was complicated legally by the involvement of the insured's Captive Insurer. The corporation insured itself with the Captive which in turn reinsured itself with the Reinsurance Market. All the duties of utmost good faith requiring disclosure of relevant facts suddenly becomes owed to the Captive. However, the Captive, in reality, only had the interest of its own parent corporation at heart and yet, it owed duties of good faith and disclosure to its Reinsurers – a real conflict of interest.

Also, the international element caused contractual issues because the multinational corporation may need separate local policies in each legal jurisdiction (e.g., France, UK, SA etc) for regulatory requirements but wanted all of its subsidiaries to have a common insurance cover. This was achieved by producing what was usually described as a Master Policy. It was intended to fill in any insurance gaps not included in the local cover.

The type of insurance policy was an adaptation of the All-Risks Policy. This was a misnomer as it did not cover all risks and only covered property loss apart from a few liability risks. It covered most insurable risks though and was the modern replacement for the old-fashioned fire policy.

I decided that there was room for a specialist but practical book dealing with this popular policy including a section on the other type of litigation evolving from these policies – subrogation. The right of subrogation occurred as a result of a legal principle whereby an insured cannot benefit twice from the same loss i.e., the insured cannot claim on its insurance and then claim the loss back from the corporation or individual causing the loss.

However, the first party property insurer can use the insured's rights of recovery to issue proceedings in the name of the insured. Those rights could be based on the potential culprit owing a duty of care to the insured or guilty of a breach of contract or even breach of duty in public law owed to the insured. Therefore, other than the right to sue itself, it was commercial litigation rather than insurance law.

With the help of an assistant to write some of the straightforward insurance chapters, I concentrated on producing a book riddled with practical examples and market practice. I renamed the policy ARPI (All Risk Property Insurance) which became a popular acronym amongst my clients. The book, published in 1996, won the BILA (British Insurance Law Association) book prize for that year.

I contributed to several other law books including a book focusing on insuring industrial machinery. I lectured regularly at client functions which I gradually came to enjoy, as should any child of the acting profession. I remember being told that only 10% of the content of a lecture was retained or even heard by the delegate; far more important was the manner of the vocal delivery, the use of hands, humour and supporting presentation. I was always able to elicit a laugh without telling a joke – just be rude about the legal profession.

I remember one of the most eccentric lectures I gave was to the Guernsey Risk Managers Association. It was quite usual to have a drinks party after a lecture. Foolishly, the organisers decided to provide alcohol before the event and only 10 minutes into the lecture, two white haired gentlemen had fallen asleep. This was not necessarily unusual, but the snoring was a little disturbing. However, I kept the talk going by dropping my books every now and again resulting in a gratifying grunt and an easy laugh from the audience.

Chapter 36
Car Life

Whilst we still had space at Martell Lodge cars flowed in and out – abundantly – for no particular reason other than a love of pretty toys. First, I went through a Bentley and Rolls Royce phase – old and cheap examples. At the end of our country lane, there was a small repair shop owned by two brothers who worked on all of our cars. However, they specialised in keeping old Rollers on the road and, knowing I was keen on cars, mentioned he had been asked to sell a 19-year-old *Rolls Royce Shadow* owner and only 18,000 miles.

I fell in love with it, particularly the lovely wood and cream leather, which was immaculate. The colour scheme was brown and bronze with that lovely silver lady. I loved it and drove it everywhere (even commuting to London). It is interesting how certain cars bring out the worst in other drivers. She was a lovely old lady and cost no more than a mid-sized Ford. However, as I travelled along the motorway I received rude signs, motorway bullying and verbal abuse. I was even asked by my partners not to drive it to the firm car park in case clients thought we earnt too much money and yet it cost about 30% of most of the vehicles owned by my colleagues – motoring ignoramuses.

So eventually I sold it, but I was now hooked and bought a *Bentley T2* in Silver Mink for local use, hoping that the winged emblem rather than the Silver Lady would bring less abuse. Believe it or not, exactly the same car (but for the emblem) in a different colour (which was movie star blue) seemed to pass the motoring public unnoticed. The interior was dark blue with velvet inserts – really over the top; Marilyn would have loved it.

Sadly, however, it was the start of a very expensive relationship with a superficially charming classic car dealer located in one of the nearby villages. The relationship was based on me dropping by for a chat and going away with another handsome looking car. I frequently part-exchanged a very good car only to find that my new car suffered from multiple faults. I would go back and part-

140

exchange that vehicle for another, suffering a huge loss. The process continued for five or six years until I purchased a brown 1980s Mercedes SL 280 with one problem after another and he actually refused to buy it back!

Then I identified another car I regretted selling – almost as much as the Charger. I had noticed over the months a rusty old vehicle hidden under a canvas tarpaulin at the Garage along the lane. Curiosity got the better of me and I made some enquiries. The Tarpaulin was ripped off and revealed a huge and tatty Bentley T1 in Brewster Green with an olive-green interior. It was such a shame to see such a fine old gentleman in parlous circumstances. The backstory was that it had been brought in for repairs and the owner had never returned to pay for it, leaving them to exercise their lien over the car. We started chatting and the idea of restoring it, something I had never done, entered the conversation. By the time I left, a deal was done.

There was to be no major change to the vehicle, just bring back some of its earlier glory. However, it was a huge vehicle as it was one of the few long wheelbase Bentley T1s, which were rare anyway; 10 times the number of Rolls Royce Shadows were built compared with the Bentley T1. I was told only about 10 LWB versions had been built. To improve its handling, we decided to fit a Harvey Bailey Handling Kit, firming up the suspension; it made a huge difference, although it would never be a sports car. I lent it to friends for weddings and one evening, we were driven back by taxi after a dinner party. ORF (the number plate) was sitting in the driveway looking very handsome and the taxi driver paid the expected compliments. He also said he was getting married the following Saturday and, without expectation, pondered on how lovely it would be to use a car like that for his wedding. In my somewhat relaxed condition, I was generosity itself and offered its use free of charge. Of course, the next morning, without actually regretting the decision, it seemed a little rash. Anyway, lovely ORF was collected and returned with no damage and several lovely photos of the young couple. ORF was a relatively long-term love affair.

Other vehicles, however, came and went for no other reason than change of change's sake. I went for the 'white period' with a white *Volvo V70 R Turbo Estate* and *Jaguar XJ12*, the latter with lovely blue upholstery and one of the last built. The V70 was a blast and very potent, used by the police as traffic chase vehicles and watching 'Wheeler Dealers' Ant Anstead, a presenter and former policeman, remembered chasing with a V70 or its predecessor. As I found out to my cost, it was great fun driving in the outside lane and vehicles pulling over believing us to be traffic cops. We were driving back late one night from Gatwick on clear roads, and I admit to being over the speed limit by close to 30mph. We heard a siren approaching from behind us and I pulled over. A very pleasant traffic officer exited from an identical V70 commenting that he had followed us for 10 miles clocking us off at 99 miles an hour. Another one mph and I lost my license automatically. I sensed he was letting me off lightly, so I gave him my effusive thanks and we moved on.

However, I always had problems with turbos. I had already owned a red Porsche 924 and was distinctly unimpressed – a low powered hatchback. However, when I went upmarket, I really went for it and possibly, I did not realise just what a rocket ship I had bought – a Porsche 944 Turbo S in black over black with a heavy-duty clutch and gearbox. With over 250bhp and 0-60 in 5.5 seconds it was, as I now realise, the world's fastest four cylinders road car. When test driving the car, the dealer had encouraged me to accelerate circling a roundabout and it seemed to have a limpet-like adhesion – in the dry. The 'S' in the name was short for 'Super' but it could equally be 'Scary'.

I later owned a cute *1997 Porsche 911 Carrera* in a lovely yellow with a blue hood and blue upholstery, but it would never match the *944 Turbo* for its instant thrill. The risk for the uninitiated was its behaviour in the wet – I was not warned. You really had to rev the rocket up to 3500revs before the Turbo clicked in and then all the power came at once – OK in the dry but problematic in the wet with no ABS or similar.

Early one Sunday morning, on a wet day, I was driving my ten-year-old to the local pool – he was my regular test car passenger. I put my foot down (probably at 50mph) and the car did a 360-degree spin and ended up in the ditch. My passenger was very brave, but I sometimes wonder whether his late development as a driver may have resulted from the accident – I was not proud of that driving.

You might have thought that was the end of the 944 in our life as it was broken in half. However, one day, a policeman arrived at the door and asked me if I had owned the same car as he was checking the history for the New Zealand police. Apparently, the car had been patched up, filled with drugs, and shipped to New Zealand. Perhaps after the black XJC, black was not my lucky colour.

The last Turbo to cause me problems was the Saab 9-5 Aero Estate. It did not match the Porsche or Volvo but the low-down power was instant in urban areas and within four weeks of ownership, I had three speeding tickets, close to a ban; another 'speedy' changeover.

Chapter 37
A Spanish Sabbatical

I was lucky enough to be allowed a 10-week sabbatical every five years. The family had just enjoyed a fine motoring holiday up the West Coast of California from San Diego to San Francisco and back, in a convertible Mustang – the only way to go.

However, when the time arrived for my first sabbatical, I intended to settle in Australia for the entire period. However, at that time, my wife found that she was unable to fly long distances and frankly, I had travelled so much globally that the prospect of a family holiday on the road did not seem much of a rest. Therefore, we visited the Costa Del Sol for a short trip to look at some cheap villas and flats – it was still the property slump, and it is always the holiday locations which suffer most from property depression. As usual with my purchases, two days was long enough to buy a pretty little villa, although I am not so sure about the bargain element; it was owned by our real estate agent! It was similar to my classic car buying, without careful consideration.

However, set in the midst of Cyprus pines, next to a house called Costa Bomb, we bought at the right time, and it was a fine holiday destination for my growing family and mother-in-law. The estate was beautifully set up, outside San Pedro, with five fine swimming pools, two minutes' walk to a beach and plenty of tennis courts.

The novelty was fine to start with but, despite appearing to be an easy holiday for a busy lawyer, every time we visited, something needed sorting (plumbing, TV, electrical bills, painting etc) and guess who ended up fixing it? So, the first few days of each visit were hard work.

As usual, the most fun times were motoring exploration on the rare occasions we left the safety of the Costa. The area around Marbella is greatly underestimated, with the old town being quite charming. The climate attracts residents from around the world with the nationalities purchasing property in phases – German, Scandinavian, Irish and Russian, by the time we left. Middle Eastern owners always bought the biggest and, of course, a fair smattering of Brits. Generally, the climate was very pleasant, although we avoided late July and August which was the only time the heat could be overpowering and the pools full of tourists. October and November could be wet with pleasant interludes, but the winter was quiet and 10 to 15°F warmers than the UK.

A little like Darwin, it attracted some eccentric residents and that included our real estate agent who shall be nameless and stateless. A very glamorous middle-aged woman, her tales could fill the pages of the Odyssey. After a few glasses of wine, the stories would start with manning the barricades of the Sorbonne in 1968 and running away to the Costa-del-Sol with a gangster. A friendship with Middle Eastern royalty and being semi-imprisoned by his princely father within a palace. The breaking off an engagement to a Bahamian alcoholic 'aristot' and doing a runner. Marrying a Mexican poet in Santa Fe and then returning to the Costa with her beautiful daughter. There were many more tales which would make a very good book or film by themselves.

The Costa was just fun, particularly Puerto Banus – the Costa's version of Monte Carlo for attracting mega yachts and a car mecca. The poor relatives (including us) showed no envy, enjoying these beautiful toys with their scantily clad occupants. A multitude of cafes offered a mix of reasonable and expensive food, but we had one favourite, Italian. One evening, a yellow Rolls Royce Corniche convertible, with white upholstery, drew up to a lovely motor yacht and the owner embarked in a white suit, split shirt, gold chains and long yellow hair. He was whisked up the gangplank by a crew of 10 young men, all dressed immaculately in matching uniforms, offering the flimsiest of salutes. The audience (including our cafe) applauded!

Our trips into inland Spain always involved problems mainly due to our very British command of the Spanish language (*dos cervezas por favor*) despite desultory Spanish lessons. In Cordoba, the whole family stayed in a backpacker's dormitory (hostel) including a 70-year-old, as I mixed up 'hotel' and 'hostel'. When visiting the white villages, I ended up driving down steep pedestrian steps because I did not understand the street sign. We stayed overnight at a lovely ancient, converted convent with an enormous Herons nest over the arched gateway where I was surprised (as was the was the waitress) by ordering roast lamb and veg for an appetiser and roast beef as a main course.

Ronda was a lovely drive up the mountains with that highland town boasting a fabulous Viaduct and Bullring. We always viewed Bullrings without bulls. Its full title was Real Maestranza de Caballería de Ronda or Bullring of the Royal Cavalry of Ronda, built in 1785 and it had an interesting museum. If you continue motoring for another two hours, you travel through glorious surreal countryside shimmering and finally, reach Seville. We always managed to visit it in the heat of summer. On one occasion, the temperature reached 47°C and we kept leaving the hotel to test the conditions. Finally, at 11:30 p.m., the temperature dropped to 33°C and we went for a walk through this lovely city.

We got into difficulty when I could not resist a little adventure off the main highway that we got into difficulty. On one occasion, we drove through a banana plantation, taking the exhaust off the manifold – it was a very noisy journey. The journey posing the greatest risk (not intentionally) was a journey through a Spanish National Park - they are not the Yorkshire Moors! We had taken a trip to Tarifa which was a windsurfing town past the Strait of Gibraltar (between Gibraltar and Cueta). (There is definitely a lack of consistency in Spain's claim over Gibraltar when it insists on remaining in control of Ceuta and Mepilla on the North African coast despite the claims of Morocco to those cities).

After a lovely morning on the wide Atlantic beaches, despite the ever-present wind and sandstorm, we headed back home but I decided to take a detour off the main highway - I am still a little vague about where we ended up but there were some river fords and a very rough, un-made road full of huge potholes. This was bad even by Australian Bush standards and we were driving a midsize rental Ford. We edged along at 5mph with two children and a 70-year-old. In the end, we were bottoming out, so all the passengers had to exit whilst the car slid through the potholes. After several miles, we finally got through. I still say motor adventures are always the most fun but perhaps only with fit adult companions.

Whilst enjoying the Spanish sunshine, home life remained the same with the continued purchase of motor cars with an ever more rapid turnover. Two manual vehicles went very quickly – a blue *Saab 16V Turbo* and red *Alfa Cloverleaf 145*. Both were great driving cars but with heavy clutches inappropriate for the 'nose-to-tail' traffic in London and so they came and went. Less understandable was the three month ownership of a lovely BMW 1987 635 CSI Highline which was an automatic and a fine car. However, for some forgotten reason, it went.

Chapter 38
A Canadian Farce

Do you remember Y2K? In a Covid world, it seems almost impossible that the computer experts and the media could predict the end of the world simply as a result of the date switching from 1999 to 2000. Of course, we now know these predictions were so wrong that, in retrospect, some suggest it was a conspiracy to ensure IT Consultants could earn a lot of money!

However, in November 1999, we all thought there would be problems and plenty that could affect industry and insurance. Unfortunately, I didn't earn any fees, but I lectured around the world in anticipation of being able to do so when catastrophe struck. Therefore, when I was asked to lecture in Toronto, I jumped at the opportunity particularly as Dad was born there and it was a country I had never visited. Unusually, Frances accompanied me so we could spend a weekend visiting Oshawa and sightseeing before a Monday return.

All went well to start with as the lecture went OK and I was pleasantly entertained by the Law Society – all part of the global insurance village. On Saturday, we started our sightseeing by a visit to the Ontario Art Museum, which incidentally, was worth a visit. On the walk back to the hotel, we passed the police headquarters. Strolling past and minding our own business, a squat muscular police officer raced out of the front door and, without explanation, grabbed my arm forcibly and dragged me into the police station with my wife berating him.

I was slammed against the front desk, still no explanation, and put into an ante-room - all I heard was 'Yes, that's the guy'. I was sat next to a cop to whom I tried to explain who I was, why I was in Toronto and to contact the organisers of the conference. I was finally pushed in front of the custody sergeant, arrested and fingerprinted. Again, there was no explanation or offer of a phone call, and I was put into a cell where I waited, completely amazed. This was not a small township in the U.S. Southern States; it was the pride of Canada. The Canadians are great at telling you how much more civilised Canada is compared to States. Well, that is not my experience and I have travelled all around the US without any problems and been treated with great courtesy.

I was not left alone for long as the same policeman entered the cell and undertook a strip search. Now this was simply gratuitous harassment as I later heard the alleged offence was minor assault. Eventually, I was visited by two plain clothes detectives and at last, I was informed of my sin – apparently, I hit a 'victim' of Caribbean heritage in the local market. I showed them my programme from the Art Gallery, explained why I was in Toronto and confirmed I had never entered any market. I also suggested they speak to my wife who I understand would not leave the Police Station despite being told to do so. I was still not given the opportunity of making a phone call. Then came my one bit of luck. One of the detectives appeared to have a Kentish accent and he volunteered that he was born in Canterbury before emigrating 20 years earlier. As he left with his partner to investigate further, he whispered that he thought a mistake had been made.

Two hours later, I was released without explanation or apology, but my new friend did say if the complainant had not been black, my treatment would have been different they were under strict orders to positively discriminate in favour of anyone other than the white Anglo Saxon.

The next day, we were off to the airport before they changed their mind, driven by the usual Canadian taxi driver, pleasantly wanting validation as to the wonders of Canada – we were politely non-committal. At the airport, the airline representative was horrified by our tale of persecution and ensured we got the next flight back, upgraded to first class.

However, this was just the beginning of this sorry saga. I was happy to put this behind me and move on. However, the conference organiser, when I explained why left early, took it upon himself to make the police pay. As a journalist, he had several contacts on the Toronto Globe and Metro Newspaper and informed them of the incident.

After a few days' investigation, an editorial was written concerning excessive use of police power, with my arrest one of the examples. There were further articles in Canada, it was mentioned in the UK Daily Telegraph, Capital Radio and finally a request by the mayor that I speak to him on a radio show. I declined but I received an apology from Toronto and an offer of a return trip to enjoy a VIP tour of Toronto – thanks but no thanks!

The finale to this farce was news from Vancouver that a 'bring back John Hanson' fund had been started up – priceless. There was a whitewash investigation by the precinct and no mention of positive discrimination, although a decision was made that strip searches required the consent of the precinct captains, so something positive arose from it.

Ironically, it did provide me with a first-class lesson of what it is like to be a victim of prejudice, mistaken identification and heavy-handed police bullying.

Chapter 39
Changes and Foreign
Lawyers

The millennium and prior year saw many changes for the Hansons. First a change of property in Spain, London, and Kent. Martell Lodge was sold for a smaller house overlooking the sea in Whitstable, The Spanish Villa was sold, and a larger flat bought in London – a minor change of lifestyle. I wanted to take the family on more Australian holidays and a larger London home to welcome the family. It meant less accommodation for cars, but I stored ORF with our garage. We became a two Jag family with the new Jaguar S-type for the family and a *Jaguar XJS V12* for me.

The S type was not exciting but made a good family car with the three litre engine in green. Now the XJS was something very special. It was one of the 1990's special editions produced to maintain sales when everyone knew they could soon be replaced. I bought it from a lovely gay couple in Isleworth and the colour scheme was very Monaco or even Puerto Banus. The bodywork was lilac with sparkling glitter and the upholstery cream with a purple piping. However, the wooden dash was the surprise as the wood was flecked with purple and gold! Please do not ask me to explain why I ever sold this one.

More important was my change at Barlows from the Reinsurance Department to start my own department with another partner to focus on the large-scale industrial risks that I had become best known for. 'Reinsurance' did not really describe my work anymore. These insurance losses could happen anywhere in the world, and I frequently had to instruct overseas lawyers in a supervisory role. Everyone has their own quirks but there were some national characteristics which only became ironed out if the foreign lawyer regularly undertook international insurance work, becoming part of the 'village'.

Many European lawyers were charming and erudite but took themselves very seriously and the firms were not operated like a US or UK law firm. Often old genteel buildings, a lack of litigation team depth and somewhat ponderous – perhaps a UK firm 30 years earlier. I would have loved to work there. German lawyers were divided into two groups: the insurance village lawyers (efficient and flexible) but there still remained many who intensely disliked the Anglo Saxon legal processes. There were significant differences in legal principles leading to different ways of thinking – coded written law as against judge made common law precedent as relied upon in the UK, the Commonwealth, and the USA. Due to a shortage of insurance lawyers on one case, I instructed a well-known elderly academic to advise on a particularly obtuse German regulation. In most of my relationships with overseas lawyers, we quickly fell into addressing each other by Christian names. I noticed that my chosen one had a title of some length e.g., Doktor Doktor Baron Von Schlosenburg. I politely asked if we could use Christian names whereupon I was informed that he expected to be addressed by his full title. I also asked that the advice be a short summary for the benefit of my client. I waited weeks for the advice which was 25 pages long with no sensible conclusion.

Sometimes, it is the legal system which controls the lawyers. In Italy, Spain, Malta, and other southern European countries litigation takes forever to complete. In the UK, the large insurance cases are determined by our streamlined Commercial Court or by Commercial Arbitration. I acted in one Maltese case which started in 1947.

Occasionally, judicial corruption could make litigation a lottery. A lawyer from a particular Middle Eastern country provided a fine legal analysis to my clients. Afterwards, he took me to one side and explained his advice was worthless because the judicial verdict would depend largely on how much we paid the judge – something my US client would not consider.

The systems and lawyers in South Africa and Australia are very similar to the UK indeed so similar that I almost moved to Australia again just about the same time I was setting up the new department. Sydney had just started its own Reinsurance Market and a well-known Sydney insurance lawyer invited me over to lecture to it. The lecture focused on the losses in the global reinsurance market over the previous 10 years; asbestos, the LMX spiral and insurance brokers' dumping poor risks. I suggested the Sydney Market was most vulnerable to the last problem. Apart from the pleasant surroundings, why would a London broker travel 10,000 miles to place a risk with a Sydney reinsurer when all he had to do was wander down the road in London? Perhaps it was because the risk would prove to be loss making. No one listened and the market closed down in five years.

I had instructed the same Sydney firm on a large mining loss, and I was invited to join their partnership. It was a close-run decision but family reasons prevented the move – we had even put a deposit on a house and arranged schooling. You should not look back but perhaps it was a lost opportunity.

I had a lot to do with South Africa in the 2000s and my local lawyers made one of the biggest marketing mistakes, I can ever remember. I had travelled to Jo'burg with my clients, and we were all invited to a barbeque at his lovely home. We all thought it was a nice gesture and we had a good evening. When I reviewed his account for the legal work it included, for the client to pay, an itemised cost of the barbeque and the time expended by his staff attending the barbeque. When my clients returned to South Africa, they pointedly asked whether they could plug in their laptops without being charged.

The lawyers I instructed in the USA were first class but again they were often hamstrung by the use of juries in very complex trials where the 'man of the street' was entirely without the expertise to determine complex issues, as indeed was the supervising judge who rarely specialised. This was a leftover from the imported English legal system in the eighteenth century. Whereas the system has changed in England so that, generally, only criminal cases used juries; in the USA, the right to a jury trial had become embedded in the Constitution and, due to generous Jury awards, it was defended by Plaintiff lawyers. Therefore, it was impossible to predict verdicts.

Sometimes, the entertainment on these trips was fun, others simply exhausting (such as a 24hr trip to Philadelphia for one meeting) and sometimes sheer torture. In particular, I remember one dinner hosted by a South Korean law firm in Seoul. There was a circular table with 10 Korean lawyers (barely speaking a word of English) and me. The meal seemed to consist of plates of Kimchi varieties and bottles of whiskey. As usual, I had to entertain in true show business fashion – goodness, it was hard work, but I became good at mime.

By contrast, I was working on an explosion of a copper smelter in Utah with witnesses spread around the world. One witness agreed to meet in Cape Town provided we would meet (together with my client, I am pleased to say) at the Camps Bay Hotel.

A lovely sophisticated, gleaming white hotel and we interviewed our witness overlooking the white beach and waves.

In the evening, it became clear our acquaintance was a player and was keen to find a club and ladies. My client and I were reluctant but to keep him happy; we found the name of a club. Our Asian taxi driver seemed very reluctant to take us there, not being a 'nice club for gentlemen'. This seemed to spur our guest on but when we arrived, I refused to go in, leaving the two of them. I took the taxi home but gave the driver a substantial sum of money and asked him to go back and discover whether my client wanted to be rescued; apparently, he did and the following day, I received some thanks.

Another witness was interviewed in Miami but Salt Lake City itself was the most interesting trip with its odd dependency on the Latter-Day Saints movements (the Mormons) but the location was lovely, surrounded by mountain peaks rising to 11,000 feet. Hugely to my surprise, I ended up instructing one of the most impressive foreign lawyers I had the pleasure to meet, and the most charming. In my job, you never knew what to expect.

Chapter 40
My New Property Insurance Department

The recovery of monies by insurers using subrogation rights depends entirely upon the quality of the insured's right of recovery against other parties which it could have exercised but for the fact it had first part property insurance; making a much easier recovery from the insurer. Some property insurers focus heavily on recoveries whereas others are for more casual but even the most dedicated struggle to achieve a better than 15% recovery.

The type of action varies hugely from suing the manufacturer/adviser of a turbine in a major South African generating power station to recovering from the Hampshire Fire Brigade following a fire destroying an office block rented by Digital. Insurers and courts do not like litigation against the fire brigades and generally, fire brigades get Court protection from civil actions seeking compensation. They may be guilty of statutory failures but even failing to turn up or late will not lead to a successful claim because courts refuse to find that emergency operations (e.g., police, coastguard, ambulance, or fire brigade) owe civil duties of care.

This is understandable as they do not want to encourage defensive behaviour by brigades when speed of thought and action is required. However, in the Hampshire Fire Brigade case, the brigade had broken one of the golden rules of fire prevention: turning off the sprinklers without first controlling the fire which the sprinklers had been holding. The brigade was not the only potential target for recovery, these included architects, builders, sprinkler installers and others. They all became defendants to the litigation and most of them settled just before the trial. The one party which refused to contribute was the fire brigade, relying on the traditional reluctance of Courts to allow such claims.

However, in addition to the clear negligence, the Brigade had proved to be very reluctant to disclose damaging internal investigation reports. Nobody likes displaying their failings in public but as far as the court was concerned, the brigade had lost its 'holier than thou' shield of protection. We still tried to settle for a small amount, but it would not budge. Our counsel was an excellent rough and tumble common law counsel, quite prepared to take the witnesses to task and we won. In essence, despite lengthy legal reasoning, the legal point was quite simple; namely in normal circumstances emergency services did not owe a duty of care unless they had volunteered to assist and taken a decision which made things worse. This had clearly happened in this instance.

Naturally, the fire brigade decided to appeal which, again, was a poor decision as these facts were so unusual. Why establish a legal principle in the court of appeal? I, then, made one of my best and hardest decisions concerning counsel. As I had said, there had to be a touch of the Theatrical Agent about the instructing solicitor and choosing the right counsel for the right court is critical.

Here, our counsel team had done an excellent job in the first trial but in an appeal on the law, I was not convinced they were right for the court of appeal – we needed another more erudite queen's counsel. My choice was frequently labelled the most intelligent man in England: Jonathan Sumption QC. He would become a member of the Supreme Court and present is the only high-profile defender of our freedoms against the current Covid restrictions.

He was a clever man, although barely interested in dialogue. He always gave the appearance of an eccentric academic rather than a commercial barrister. In this case, however, he was brilliant, commanding the law, the judges, the 12 or so counsel and just about everything else. It was a tour de force and, as I heard muttered on the quiet by another Counsel, 'if Sumption says it so it must be so'. Sadly, therefore, the Hampshire taxpayer became liable for a £20 million increase in rates, one of whom was a grumbling fellow partner!

The other primary source of work for the department was the defence of claims by insurers and reinsurers they had decided to reject for insurance policy reasons. One of the most interesting losses concerned a Borax open pit mine in California where one side of the mine had slipped causing huge rock falls. There were a variety of potential defences for the insurers; including whether the claim was excluded under the policy and whether there had been non-disclosure of relevant information by the mining corporation.

I had never realised that the use of Borax was so hugely versatile and valuable, although it is now banned in the UK as potentially hazardous to health

– this was not the case in 2000. It was used in detergents, cosmetics, enamel glaze, fire retardant, anti-fungal, fiberglass, an agent in cooking and insecticides.

There were various meetings in California including an occasion where lawyers, clients and experts posed as a tourist party to obtain a better view of the alleged slippages. Any dispute would be resolved in Australia. There were several reasons for this peculiarity. First, the insured was a mining company with its main corporate office registered in Melbourne. Second it had set up a captive insurance company located first in Singapore and Bermuda which accepted the direct risk from its own parent company and the reinsured a major part of the risk partly into the Australian insurance market but largely to my client, an American owned industrial property insurer but with an Australian subsidiary. Therefore, the insurance/reinsurance contract contained an Australian jurisdiction clause requiring disputes to be resolved in Victoria.

Therefore, the contractual chain was as follows:

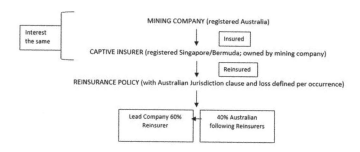

There were all sorts of problems concerning poor contractual documents, but the harder task was to persuade the captive insurer to use all of the defences available to it as it clearly had a conflict of interest (hoping its parent company would succeed). However, there was one good defence which separated the captive from its reinsurers. It is usual for any insured and reinsured to retain an amount which it pays itself and, in this case, the captive had reinsured its parent company on a different basis than the cover provided by the reinsurers. Therefore, the captive retained part of the risk and the loss. The captive reinsurer had agreed in the reinsurance contract to pay a specified amount per occurrence. Occurrence phrasing meant that several losses might be added together and trigger only one deductible had to be paid by the captive. (The amounts below are hypothetical – in reality, they were larger.)

Reinsurers argued that the rock falls had been three separate rock falls whereas the Captive argued there had been one slippage. This made a huge difference in that if the incident had been a £30 million loss with three occurrences, the £10 million retention would be triggered three times meaning the Reinsurers would have to pay very little. On the other hand, if it was determined there was only one occurrence this would mean one retention and the Reinsurers (including my client) would have to pay £20 million.

We all met in Melbourne and my client decided that it would rely on my advice that there had been 3 occurrences, settle with the Insured (with the captive approval) and arbitrate the number of occurrences with captive.

There was a degree of flexibility because a standalone arbitration Agreement was agreed separately from the Reinsurance Contract. This allowed a commercial and flexible form of the resolution of disputes using arbitrators rather than Judges. This was critical because a term of the settlement agreement was that the matter should be resolved in eight weeks – it would take three to four years if a court had to be used. Therefore, each party had to find and organise an arbitrator (two UK QCs), an umpire (a Sydney Judge) and experts on mining and geology all in eight weeks near the Christmas holiday.

Perhaps it was the attraction of Australia in the English winter which made it all possible. During the arbitration, many reasons were given for the rock falls by the Captive leading to our Geotech experts mocking up a spoof front page of the Sun Newspaper (hanging on my study wall) with a picture of a U.S. bomber and headline:

'BORAX CLAIMS U.S. BOMBS CAUSED SLOPE FAILURES'

Expert evidence was called on both sides with the Captive arguing that within geological parameters a couple of months between each visual rockfall did not stop it from being one occurrence because they were all linked and never stopped moving. Our argument was simple: if you asked an observer and left him standing there for 3 months would he identify one or three incidents?

In the end, we won the arbitration by a majority of two to one and my clients were barely required to pay anything. This was my 'Australian Period' with pipeline, gold mining claims, a defective smelter and even an insurance broking claim in Adelaide where I managed to watch an Australia versus West Indies test match, meet some old Darwin friends, and visit the Barossa Valley.

In all of these cases, the most enjoyable part was learning in detail about the various industries – turbines, mines of various sorts etc. I became a temporary 'expert' on electrolysis, pots, anodes, electrodes for aluminium smelters (even enjoying the most boring and longest eight hour lecture on pots by an expert), the largest open coal mine located in North Scandinavia, smelters, and various manufacturing plants from food to IT equipment.

I have strayed a long way from motor cars for which I apologise.

Chapter 41
Besotted with Australia

A reluctant exile from Australia, the many mining cases I had collected, regular business visits and our continued friendships started me thinking about life after the law. Life had not been without pleasures in England but, for retirement, sun, and space, motoring around his huge island seemed very attractive. Holidays and two sabbaticals were spent determining whether Australia was our future: part of the reason for selling the Spanish villa.

Back to motoring holidays; the first to Darwin and Cairns. At last, we properly explored North Queensland, although we were now tourists rather than adventurers. We 'enjoyed' a crocodile challenged golf course in Port Douglas, giving a different meaning to water hazards. Canoeing in the Daintree rainforest or snorkelling with 200 tourists on the Great Barrier Reef were delightful but perhaps a touch Disneyland.

On another trip, Noosa Heads had not lost its charm. Slightly north of Noosa, Fraser Island provided a touch of danger that had been missing. I had driven past the Island on several occasions but as we had hired a four-wheel-drive we decided to visit for a day. It was a dangerous but a unique ecological location and by no means limited in size. It was the largest sand island (although lying on bedrock) in the world being 76 miles long and 14 miles wide.

The island was riddled with mini rough tracks, but the highway consisted of the eastern beach and doubled up as an airstrip. The island was packed and dripping with aggressive wildlife. The sea was protected by fearsome rip currents and by shark colonies patrolling the inland waters. Therefore, sea swimming was not recommended but this was compensated for by over 100 freshwater lakes. For the swimmer, luckily, the lakes were contaminated by excessive organic acid which deterred other wildlife from permanently inhabiting these crystal-clear ponds.

We knew all of this in advance and decided to take the shortest ferry journey (of the two alternatives) from Inskip to the Southern point on the island. However, as we drove the Toyota Hilux up the beach we caught sight of packs of dingoes – dog-like wolves. We later discovered, there were 30 odd packs on Fraser Island, a poisonous spider for every square metre, a few saltwater crocodiles, and a fine variety of snakes, including the death adder and taipan.

As the Chamberlain case had proved, dingoes were a danger. We spent the day discovering the amazing variety of ecological systems, rumbling through the rainforest, eucalyptus and the oldest sand dune system in the world, including the Coloured Sands and Rainbow Gorge. There was a lot to see, and we were running short of time, but we had to have a swim in Lake McKenzie, the largest of the lakes. Suddenly we realised we only had an hour to reach the last ferry leaving the island. Jolting through the rainforest and rollicking down the beach in our Toyota two cab Hilux we were horrified to notice that the tide was catching us up. We were constantly watching whether we would be swallowed up. Unfortunately, near the ferry point the tide had washed away the beach and there was no way we could get to the ferry. We gave it up as a lost cause and turned around to find we were stuck in the wet sand. Shoving it free, we tried to cut across the Peninsula through the dunes only to get buried in the soft sand. We got out and dug out the rear wheels and placed deadwood under them.

Desperate, soaked, and sandy we freed the vehicle and piled in for a race to beat the waves. Turning inland, we found the only catering establishment, and, despite our disreputable appearance, we were allowed to hire a basic self-catering cabin.

The restaurant was the only one in Australia which would have allowed entry for this misbegotten bunch. However, following beer, red wine, T-bone steaks and salads, we were feeling more the thing and later wandered past skulking dingoes, to be serenaded by howling in the morning. I have always kept a note of the occasional attack on the island and thinking here but for the grace of God…

On another occasion, we spent a very wet November in Byron Bay. We also undertook the journey from Melbourne to Sydney and returned, repeating earlier journeys in my younger days. It was pleasant but of course did not have the youthful novelty. It was on this trip that we almost bought the little house in Mainly an omission I always regret with its idyllic views over Sydney Harbour.

In this period, we were still buying and selling houses and cars. We had moved quickly from Whitstable to an Oast House with twin roundels next to an Anglo-Saxon churchyard in Wickhambreaux. Very quickly, we wondered whether the 1840 Oast had been built on the graveyard. The sellers were a young Welsh couple who had lived in a caravan on site for four years, renovating and crafting a Tolkien like home but curiously dark and spooky – instead of the Adams family, it was the Hanson family. Actually, on reflection, I can definitely see Morticia in my wife and with my Latin moustache, perhaps I had a touch of Gomez.

The following accounts are my evidence of ghostly manifestation (our X Files). First, every time one turned the lights off on the three floors, 10 minutes later they were on again. One centrally heated bedroom was so cold no one would sleep in it. Family members swore they saw ghostly shapes passing through the graveyard and belongings constantly went missing. In our 12-month residence at the Oast House, we lost a much-loved close family member, we were cursed with serious floods, a plague of rats, an infestation of flies, the Twin Towers disaster and I collapsed from overwork. We decided on a rearrangement of property and lifestyle.

As an aside, I am sure that Frances triggered these manifestations because at Martell Lodge I was told that, whilst I was away, early in the morning, ghostly horses and the clink of weaponry were heard in the fields. It resulted in children, mother-in-law and dogs hiding out in the same bedroom. I will continue with this ghostly conjecture by describing a failed purchase of a fifteenth Century house in Minster. It was a very old property with a Georgian Facade and on inspection both my wife and I felt very uncomfortable. So, I instructed my conveyancer, much to his amusement, to insert in the preliminary enquiries the following question:

'During the course of your residency have you ever experienced ghostly manifestation or arranged an exorcism or similar event?'

The answer was yes to both questions – no wonder they were moving to Spain. Our next move was to a much more cheerful but very odd marine residence described as a 'Tower Bungalow'. A collection of these bungalows was built on the cliff top in Birchington facing the North Sea. They were notable for having a single storey building with a small two or three storey extension, known as the Tower. They were the earliest bungalows built in the UK. These were bungalows with a difference as they were built in the 1880s and in a very early rustic arts and crafts style. Ours had a large dining room with a brick fireplace capable of roasting a suckling pig on a spit overlooking the North Sea.

Battered and beaten by the sea over 100 years, the house required a major restoration exercise which was made aesthetically difficult due to various unattractive extensions and the loss of garden to the sea together with the intrusion of ugly modern bungalows built after the war. It is ironic that these attractive innovative designs (following the Bengali design originally built for the employees of the British Raj) should result in an attractive seaside village being overwhelmed by the post-war bungalow intrusion.

The building of a sea wall below the cliff had put the sea erosion on hold but not before half of the garden had washed away. On buying by the sea, it is easy to get carried away with the splendid views forgetting the disadvantages such as the destructive winter winds, the nesting and aggressive Seagulls, the constant need to renew the exterior decoration and the truly awful smell from the seaweed in the summer heat.

In the end, we did not entirely escape the ghostly intervention - no one wanted to sleep in the 'Tower Bedroom'. We discovered later that someone had committed suicide there.

Motor cars came and they went. My Bentley (ORF) came out of storage briefly at the Oast House but had to be sold on our move to the coast. Two lousy cars from our unreliable dealer followed – a *Range Rover* and finally the *1977 Mercedes SL* was. The end of an expensive relationship. A smart blue *BMW 3 Series estate car* and a fine maroon Daimler Super V8 (with a fantastic supercharged 400bhp engine, managing a refined 0-60mph in five seconds or thereabouts) were the next purchases. Cream piped leather upholstery and fine-grained wood. It was a favourite, but the restricted driveway resulted in numerous scrapes. So, it was onto a double Mercedes purchase – a bright blue Mercedes E-Class Estate and a lovely 'hairdressers' *CLK320 convertible* in emerald green with a pale green hood. The colours hooked me!

Chapter 42
Looking for a Change

The change of lifestyle resulted in buying a bigger London flat to house more visits from family and at last enjoying the attractions offered by our capital city. Eventually, we moved the family home to an easily maintained Victorian house in Canterbury. However, it was now 20 years since I moved back to England and into Barlow Lyde and Gilbert – I would never have believed that I could be so stable. I suppose one reaches a stage in life when a certain income is required to support a family and one law firm is much the same as another.

As far as cars were concerned, space was limited, and my wife drifted into the small car syndrome – which I have always hated driving. So, we were rarely without a car similar to a *Yaris,* or a *VW Polo* and I became a Lexus man just as my father was a Jaguar man. Over the next 14 years, I was rarely without a *Lexus RX* and occasionally, the fine *Lexus 450 H.* The colour range included two navy blue, two silver clack and lovely cerulean blue and a crimson and silver version for the 450H. So why Lexus rather than a German car or a Jaguar? First and foremost, they were better made and when I started to buy them the hybrid technology was advanced; although I have always considered its electric motor is the equivalent of a supercharger rather than a green addition.

This was particularly obvious in the 450H which boasted 340bhp and could achieve 0-60 in 5.7 seconds but still managed 40 miles per gallon. Uniquely, the mpg did not differ between town and motorway driving. The finish inside was lovely and tasteful, compared with a Bentley. As always, I liked the fact that the pundits underrated them – what did they know?

The RX was not a heavy-duty four-wheel drive but my days of adventure treks were over. It was a very comfortable load carrier which became necessary as we spent more and more time driving to Scotland. The drive through England is truly awful whichever route you take – in the end, we settled for the A1 with a stopover in Durham; halfway from our favourite destination - the 'Black Isle'.

Located just over Kessock Bridge, north of Inverness, it was neither black nor an island, but it was watery. It is an extended peninsular terminating to the west with a small town as lovely as its name, Beauly, and to the east the equally lovely Cromarty. Its borders are the Cromarty Firth, the Eastern Moray Firth, and the southern Beauly Firth.

Perhaps 'black' because viewed from Inverness the rich black soil provides a fine base for agriculture and colours the peninsular black. For such a small peninsular it provides a variety of landscape and views particularly North towards Ben Wyvis, more ridge than a mountain. From Chanonry Point, outside Fortrose, one can enjoy the spectacle of the dolphin pod, with over 200 members frolicking in the Moray Firth or take a boat trip from Cromarty. On one occasion, we missed the tourist boat and, whilst hanging about on the jetty, part of the pod ventured to about 50ft from us and provided a free performance.

Cromarty is so special that we almost bought a house converted from the cottage hospital. Earlier interaction with ghostly apparitions had not converted me to a believer but I was still uneasy about a holiday home with an old morgue attached.

For such a small town, it was the birthplace of several noted academics and writers, including Sir Thomas Urqant, Hugh Miller, and the holiday home of Ian Rankin (the well-known creator of the Inspector Rebus series) who lives in one of the lovely merchant houses. The Black Isle features in his book, 'Standing in Another Man's grave' and his hero bores for Scotland on the subject of the A9 road – the only north-eastern route through the Southern Highlands to Inverness. The views are lovely on the trip, but you do not need a fast car - with speed limits and tourists to overcome. The merchant houses interact with mini fishermen's cottages. Historically a fishing port with its own local Northern Scots dialect. Its last speaker, Bobby Hogg, died in 2012 and, coincidentally, the owner of the house we contemplated buying was his daughter.

This delightful fishing village, however, is currently blighted by the Cromarty Firth being the Scottish graveyard for returned oil rigs. When we first visited, they were a novelty, and we trendily appreciated the juxtaposition of highland views with heavy industry. However, every time we returned the numbers had increased and now, they dominate the landscape – the spectator may as well be on the Clyde unless he or she has turned the corner to look east towards the guardians of the Firth entrance: 'The Suitors'.

All of this steel and iron contrasts oddly with wonderful marine life such as dolphins, seals and minke whales. The Firth is even visited by humpback whales and basking sharks. However, historically, this wonderful anchorage has been home to far more glamorous and deadly visitors being a primary base in the North for the Royal Navy and a training based in the Second World War for sea planes – including my favourite, the Sunderland.

The Black Isle boasted its own small 'beach resorts' like no other in Rosemarkie and Fortrose. The cold water of the Moray Firth lap gently onto little beaches very similar to some lakes in Switzerland. The Isle also provides a fine base for adventures across Scotland to the west coast, as Scotland is so narrow the journey only takes a couple of hours. Alternatively, one can drive north into the truly magical Sutherland wilderness.

The Lexus RX was ideal for these journeys although at home I still bought an occasional less sensible vehicle, like the yellow and blue Porsche Carrera mentioned earlier or the yellow and black Mini Convertible Works. However, despite these distractions, I was still searching for a 50 plus return to 'youthful' adventures.

Chapter 43
Back to the Tropics

56 years old, two or three stone heavier and weighed down further with family and possession. Was I ready for another tropical adventure (trying to relive my youth)? Opportunities were limited for a lawyer close to 'city' retirement age but out of the blue, the relatively new Barlows Singapore office decided it needed greater depth for its insurance and reinsurance expertise. No one could question my expertise, but I was not a first choice because of my age. Indeed, I discovered, unsurprisingly, that most Singapore imports were aged between 30 and 40 and, for my future credibility, it would always be difficult to persuade clients that I would remain longer than my two year contract. It was clearly a quasi-retirement project.

However, there were no other 'takers'. The firm was going through a fragile period and younger partners were reluctant to take a risk whereas I wanted any risk! I also welcomed the change from an equity partner to a salaried partner – the former opened a partner up to liabilities, the latter did not!

What did I know about Singapore? I had stayed over for a few stopovers but was usually too jetlagged to take much in. However, I always stayed in the Shangri La Hotel in Orchard Road. I remembered the tropical lagoon-style pool and the Singapore Noodles. So, when looking for accommodation we were pleasantly surprised to find that the hotel had four types of accommodation – the economy hotel, the first-class hotel, short term self-catering flats and long term (annual) residences. It was one of the latter residences that we settled upon.

I knew something about the history of Singapore and in particular, its development from a fishing village by Sir Stamford Raffles in 1818. He was determined to establish another port/colony to challenge the Dutch in the east positioned on the Straits of Malacca. Despite being smelly, lawless and with a horrible humid climate its establishment still has a certain romance. Labourers and merchants moved in from China, Malaya, and India. With no tax being a free port, free trade flourished between European and Asian merchants, with the Chinese in the middle taking a cut.

Steamships increased the trade, and the two opium wars encouraged a flood of Chinese immigrants. However, despite flourishing economically, its administration was appalling, encouraging drugs, gambling, and prostitution. The administration was the result of a historical accident. It was originally established by the East India Company (EIC) not the British government. After the Anglo-Dutch Treaty 1824, Singapore was amalgamated into the Straits settlement by the EIC which bizarrely became a subdivision of the President of Senegal in British India – 3000 miles away.

The increasing trade and the growing importance meant that it was time for the British government in 1864 to invest its own money and set up Singapore as a Crown Colony under the supervision of the Colonial Office, which continued until our pitiful defence of the colony from the Japanese attack in the Second World War.

I also realised that the climate would be hot and humid but without realising how hard this would be for an 'older' couple. Darwin had been bad enough, but it at least had a pleasant 'Dry Season'. The climate in Singapore did not really change, being so close to the equator, with daytime temperatures of 35°F and 80% – 100% humidity. It was so humid and wet that my wife could not walk down Orchard Road without falling down with visits to the hospital on two occasions.

It was impossibly expensive to buy and run cars in Singapore and so with plentiful taxis we decided to remain car-free, much to my disappointment. However, it did not prevent the wealthy from collecting the most extraordinary collection of super cars which, in the night, roared around the city creating their own Grand Prix Track – Lamborghinis, Ferraris being first and foremost.

The taxis were good value for the gossip you heard from the drivers – perhaps the only place you could receive an honest opinion of the benevolent autocracy which was described as democratic. Singapore was ruled by the PAP (People's Action Party) and it had been true to its name. The Second World War had devastated this tiny island by the brutality of its conquerors, evidenced by the use of Changi prison as effectively a concentration camp. The messages left by relatives of the inmates are truly heart rending and this ignores the treatment of the local population, particularly the Chinese. Why do neighbours so often fight amongst themselves?

The failure of Britain to defend its far eastern colonies and the lack of finance to repair the damage resulted in the 1950s saw the inevitable move towards independence. Independence arrived in 1963 and Singapore merged with Malaysia. Differences led to a peaceful demerger in 1965, leaving a small and vulnerable island but blessed with its own hero statesman – Lee Kuan Yew. It is very easy to denounce his legacy as a dictatorship, but this would be to ignore the transformation of this impoverished colonial leftover into one of the safest, best armed, economically successful, and socially integrated nations in the world.

How did an individual and his party achieve this result? Well, it helped being small and without natural resources. There was no choice but to become a low tax, merchant, and manufacturing driven centre. It always looked ahead for the next niche industry to add to its core – shipbuilding, tourism, then pharmaceuticals, electronics and, by the time I arrived, the service industries such as banking, and insurance has been added. Indeed, it was even far-sighted enough to see that international dispute resolution was an opportunity for Singapore to become the primary location for commercial arbitration in the Far East.

The promotion of arbitration had several consequences in Singapore, on which I was asked to lecture. I also lectured on insurance and reinsurance in Singapore, Hong Kong, and Kuala Lumpur. However, as a natural resolver of disputes, my lack of admission to the local court system proved to be highly frustrating and, indeed, it was the one major omission to Singapore's open capitalist and free trade principle. In this case personal self-interest won out amongst the many lawyers in the PAP – they created a closed shop even worse than the Channel Islands. So too old, too hot, and professionally frustrated this was never going to be a long tenure.

Without doubt, the best part of our brief sojourn was staying in the wonderful Shangri La Residences. Across the road from the hotel, we enjoyed our own lovely pool and a three bedroomed and air conditioned flat with its own roof terrace and hot tub - just what you do not need in the tropics. As we also had full use of the hotel facilities (including the other pools) my wife enjoyed the gratis champagne and canapés served every afternoon in the first-class part of the hotel – not strictly for the benefit of the flat residents but, strangely, she got on very well with the head waiter.

Indeed, the hotel staff managed to make it feel like a very glamorous home without the patronising starchiness of English luxury hotels – welcoming without ever being too familiar. We felt very spoilt – we were very spoilt. If you are in Singapore on a Sunday never miss the breakfast buffet and at the Shangri La, it was fabulous, with numerous different food stations from Italian to Japanese food. It is, therefore, unsurprising we had numerous overseas guests to indulge in the fabulous food in Singapore.

Of course, the colonial architectural heritage had been largely torn down, replaced by multi-storeyed blocks – very glamorous for the wealthy. However, the locals had not done so badly by most owning their own flats. The system forced them to accept a purchase price from a central fund which they were obliged to pay back over their lifetime. However, we can learn a lot from the Singapore government's management of social housing which has resulted in 90% of the Singaporeans owning their own homes. Each separate high-rise township is independent with services and shopping malls – unlike in the UK where developers get away with new developments devoid of any supporting infrastructure. Prices are a third of the open market and supported by a control fund.

Maintenance is ensured and vandalism is limited – it is simply not worth the penalties. Graffiti criticising the PAP is enough to warrant a local headline and painted out within 24 hours. This sums up Singapore – everything works but to do so requires a limitation of personal expression. Therefore, in retirement they might own their residence and have a small capital sum. Indolence and ill-discipline were not tolerated, punishments were severe, and crimes (however minor) identified by highly efficient surveillance. We hardly noticed a policeman – they were, allegedly, ensconced in bunkers viewing on screens. Basically, if you worked hard and obeyed the rules you were OK – for the sick and poor Singapore may not be the best place to reside.

The proximity of Singapore to Darwin was a great advantage – only four hours direct flight which made a long weekend possible. We took advantage on several occasions together with a longer trip to the North Island, New Zealand. It also included a trip back to London and at the partners meeting I gathered just how much mismanagement had led to the firm struggling to survive. I felt guilty enjoying such a generous package in Singapore and offered up my resignation. It was agreed that I would return to London as a consultant.

So, Singapore was probably too little too late and, without doubt, my last hurrah. There is a time and place for everything – the Tropics is a place for Anglo-Saxons still enjoying their youth.

Chapter 44
Retirement and Reflections

Retirement was forced on me at 59. First, through a decade of poor firm management, it was close to collapse and forced to merge with a firm which had been our major competitor for the last 50 years. I played no part in the debacle other than by default. I did castigate myself for not playing a larger part in central management over the years. It had never appealed to me, beyond managing my own team, and I was happy to focus on the Law. Frequently, I buried my head in the sand when daft decisions were made, of which there were plenty. A profession as a business is an odd beast because frequently a partner is the **product** (the legal advice), the **shareholder** and the **manager**. They are not trained as managers; they rarely relinquish power to those who are trained to be managers and frequently the most able partners are more interested in the law and do not understand the distinction between administration and management (too frequently confused by these amateurs).

Late in my career, I was not interested in joining our competitor in what was, in truth, a takeover; its culture was entirely different to Barlow Lyde and Gilbert. I had plans elsewhere but then the second factor kicked in. After reasonably good health all my life (apart from TB), I was incapacitated by one health problem after another. Therefore, as I write in the 'Time of Covid', my life was not changed hugely by this virus, life has simply become smaller and smaller.

It will not surprise the reader to be told that my retirement plans included travel and possibly living in Australia either full or part time. Long distance travel became impossible and, indeed ironically, I have almost become paranoid over travel overseas. We sold up our flat and seaside home and bought a Victorian pile in Canterbury and that became my island. I was, for the first time in my life, stationary.

Pleasures have been the small ones, such as breakfast at the Kent Cricket Club and breaks away usually headed north to Scotland. These gradually became spoilt by the SNP cult with the Scots becoming less and less welcoming. It is particularly sad for my wife who is a Gordon with a Scottish heritage dating back to the thirteenth Century. My father was brought up entirely in Scotland from the age of 5 to 17. Great Britain is a tiny island, and it is faintly absurd to believe that a tiny state, with a GNP and population about the same size as Northwest England, will be successful as an independent nation. With only 8% of Great Britain's economic output, it can only ever be a supplicant principality; bullied by the EU. Whether you are a Brexiteer or a Remainer, the next 10 years will be an adventure for the UK.

Of course, no one likes being sick, but I was able to reflect on the fact that I had been adventurous in my youth. Repeating yet again my father's mantra, 'You attack life so hard, John, you will be worn out at 60' – I didn't quite make it. Mind you, this was really the 'pot calling the kettle black'.

Car buying continued but began to demonstrate a lack of rationality triggered by boredom - in other words when in doubt buy a car. A list is probably the best way of dealing with the multiple purchases. My first retirement purchase illustrates how low I had sunk by buying a Toyota Prius, although shortly after, I added a rather fine black *Jeep Wrangler* to it. My current collection demonstrates a change in philosophy – a Black *Mercedes AMG CLK 350*, a 1993 Crystal green *Mercedes SL500*, a 2010 *Lexus RX* in a lovely cerulean blue and white upholstery and a grey mean-looking Audi A1 with a little beast of an engine. Of course, I cannot drive any of them.

In between these extremes, we owned a Saab Aero Convertible (the celebration model) which was a rattle trap, a VW Polo, and an Alfa Mito. We owned a variety of four wheel drive vehicles for our trips to Scotland including another Lexus RX, a Lexus NX and two VW Touregs (grey and white). A pretty VW Beetle Convertible dressed in pale blue came and went.

I indulged in two lovely Alfa Spiders of the last generation – I do not know why I sold the later one (nuts). They were both blessed with a lovely 3.2 litre engine and an automatic for the lazy elderly driver. It is the most comfortable and relaxing small convertible ever produced by Alfa. The seats are generous and the engine underdeveloped but still responsive. They are, of course, rare and I probably sold the best two existing in the UK – idiot!

I then bought on spec, when I was not 'all there', a 12-year-old Porsche Cayenne with 90,000 miles in a fabulous marine blue. It was not a bad car, but it was at a stage when it was always being fixed. Just as I had sorted it out, I became impatient, and part-exchanged it for the Lexus 450H – another lovely car in crimson and cream which I sold within three months.

I am exhausted after that list and, although the best car of my current crop, I shall probably sell the lovely Mercedes SL500 when the markets open up. This was the best period for Mercedes engineering and the V8 500 the best engine – in 1992, its 0-60mph was about six seconds even though it is built like a mini-tank. I think the technical description is 'over engineered'. The CLK makes a better noise with a fabulous AMG exhaust but the most fun is the Audi with a raspy little supercharged and turbocharged engine it holds the road like a Mini Cooper.

I have purposely avoided discussion of friends and family in this AUTO-Biography as this was intended to be the memories of cars and the life of one baby boomer enjoying the freedoms available. I have been lucky enough to enjoy one of the most affluent and peaceful periods in our history. I have taken more risks than most, but it always seemed as though the dice were loaded in my favour. The last eight years have been my comeuppance.

My luck was to be given a good education and being brought up by parents who survived a world war to pass on the benefits of hard work. There were no easy handouts for me, which most middle-class parents donate to their children (including mine) currently.

Since leaving home at 18, I have provided for myself and those close to me and even during the past years I have supported our late maturing children. I have grumbled, as do all parents but without some sacrifice and family to support life would have been pretty thin gruel. The 'Time of Covid' has been pretty lousy for everyone but, with some decent leadership, I have enough confidence in this country to be optimistic about its prospects. Initially, I was ambivalent about Brexit but as time wore on, I was so unimpressed with the negativity oozing from the remainer camp that, like much of my life, I became excited by the possibility of a new adventure.

I am not excited by the prospect of the substitution of the combustion engine by electrical power. It is unrealistic to expect the national grid to power every vehicle in the UK - it will neither be green nor practical to switch completely to electricity on a certain date. Graduated car tax could be introduced to deter purchasing polluting vehicles and, in the meantime, there could be a focus on vehicle self-generation such as solar power, hydrogen fuel cells and others. As usual, facile politicians, ill-informed and desperate to impress family, friends and girlfriends make ill-considered gestures of greenness without proper consultation. Policy is made on 'the hoof' – does this remind you of the initial response to Covid?

As a baby boomer, I say farewell to the combustion engine and the freedom offered to a generation which we enjoyed as a result of the hardships of our parents and grandparents. My motto could be: 'I made the most of my luck!'

9 781398 467163